J

Crisis Communications Handbook

First Edition

Louie Fernandez

Martin Merzer

WWW. MASSHOME.
COM

Jane's Information Group

Editorial Project Management
Content Developer: *Jessica Duda*

Editorial
Content Developer: *Rennie Campbell*
Content Developer: *Jim Tinsley*

Production
Group Content Manager: *Anita Slade*
Global Production Services Manager: *Jane Lawrence*
Content Editing Manager: *Jo Agius*
Production Editors: *David Blake, Chris Bridge, Diana Burns*

Front Cover Design
Senior Design Manager: *Steve Allen*
Content Developer: *Jessica Duda*

Administration
Content Development Manager: *Ian M Synge*
Chief Content Officer: *John Boatman*
Chief Executive Officer: *Alfred Rolington*

Published by Jane's Information Group

1340 Braddock Place, Suite 300
Alexandria, Virginia 22314-1657, United States
Tel: (+1 703) 683 3700
Fax: (+1 703) 836 0297
e-mail: info@janes.com

Printed in the UK

Registered with the Library of Congress
Cataloging-in-Publication Data available upon request

ISBN 0-7106-2596-0

Publisher's Note

Jane's would like to thank the authors of *Jane's Crisis Communications Handbook*:

Louie Fernandez, lead editor of *Jane's Crisis Communications Handbook*, is Senior Bureau Chief for Public Affairs with Miami-Dade County's Fire Rescue (MDFR) and Office of Emergency Management (OEM). Chief Fernandez has contributed to more than 25 OEM activations in his 8 years as a Public Information Officer (PIO), including the 1998 Carnival Cruise Lines ship fire, and served as primary spokesperson for the 1996 ValuJet Airlines crash and the 1997 Fine Air crash. He standardized MDFR-OEM's media relations operating procedures and created a modern video-production and press center serving the major local, national and international news affiliates. He was lead instructor for emergency-response training missions in Latin America for the US State Department-sponsored Bureau of International Programs (BIP). Chief Fernandez is a 15-year veteran of MDFR and was awarded the State of Florida Fire Chiefs' PIO of the year in 1996.

Martin Merzer, is a Senior Writer for *The Miami Herald*. Over the course of his career at *The Associated Press* and *The Miami Herald,* Mr Merzer has covered many crises ranging from the September 11 attacks on the World Trade Center and the Pentagon, to the civil war in Beirut, the famine in Ethiopia and the Sudan, Hurricane Andrew in South Florida, the Gulf War and the assassination of Israeli Prime Minister Yitzhak Rabin. Mr Merzer's coverage of Hurricane Andrew in 1992 and the Elian Gonzalez case in 2000 contributed to the *The Miami Herald's* Pulitzer Prize awards. Mr Merzer is the author of *The Miami Herald Report: Democracy Held Hostage*, St. Martin's Press published June 2001.

In addition to the authors, the following leant their considerable expertise and experience in crisis communications issues during the development and final review of the handbook:

Patrick Alesi
Vice-President, Business Continuity Management, Lehman Brothers, New York, NY

Randy Atkins
Senior Media Relations Officer, National Academy of Engineering, Washington, DC

Zvi Bar'el
Middle east analyst for *Ha'aretz Daily,* Tel Aviv, Israel

Captain Joseph Della Vedova
Media Relations Trainer, US Air Force, Pentagon, Arlington, VA

Lt Col Bob Domenici
WMD/Homeland Security Officer, Division of Military & Naval Affairs, New York Army National Guard

Dr Frances Edwards-Winslow, CEM
Director of Emergency Preparedness, San Jose, CA

Rebecca Fleischauer
Senior Public Affairs Officer, KSA-Plus Communications, Arlington, VA

Tara Hamilton
Public Affairs Manager, Metropolitan Washington Airports Authority, Washington, DC

Commander Jim McPherson
Chief, Media Relations, US Coast Guard, Washington, DC

Debra Miller
Principal, Citigate Sard Verbinnen, New York, NY

Rapheal Perl
Specialist in International Terrorism Policy, Congressional Research Service, Washington, DC and Study Director: Committee on Combating Terrorism: Prioritizing Vulnerabilities & Developing Mitigation Strategies, National Academy of Engineering, Washington, DC

Bonnie Piper
Deputy Director of Media Relations, Office of Public Affairs, US Environmental Protection Agency, Washington, DC

Barbara Reynolds
Crisis Communications Specialist, Center for Disease Control and Prevention, Atlanta, GA

Gary Tuchman
National Correspondent, CNN, Atlanta, GA

Paul Viollis
Managing Director, Security Services Practice, Citigate Global Intelligence & Security, New York, NY

Table of Contents

Chapter 4: Response procedures checklists

Chapter 5: Gathering and verifying information

Chapter 6: Messages and strategy

Chapter 7: Engaging key stakeholders

Chapter 8: Working with the media

Chapter 9: Post-incident management

Chapter 10: Appendices

CHAPTER 1: STRATEGIC OVERVIEW

CHAPTER 1: STRATEGIC OVERVIEW

1.1 Introduction

The chaos of a crisis can affect any private or public organization impacting an array of stakeholders – those the crisis affects and from whom the organization requires support. In broad terms, a crisis is any unexpected incident **potentially** upsetting an organization's employees, customers, operations, reputation, finances or the local/national community.

Any organization can encounter an emergency at any time which requires **effective communications during and after the incident.** Crises, such as workplace or school violence, transport accidents, terrorist attacks or corporate scandals, differ in cause, severity and consequence. Crises, however, share certain characteristics:

◆ **Confusion surrounds the scene** but slowly evolves into some degree of order
◆ **On-scene response is critical** as it contributes to the chain reaction of events and media coverage of the organization's capabilities
◆ **Events escalate** as challenges continue to confront the response team possibly attracting media speculation
◆ **Information is initially conflicting** and tends to arrive in sudden bursts

◆ **Public interest** soars initially, especially for reassurance, and then tends to diminish
◆ **External influence is unavoidable** as reporters, politicians, competitors, commentators, regulators and others – many of whom know little about the organization(s) involved – comment on the response and impact the overall message. This in turn, influences public perception of the response effort.

1.2 Role of crisis communications

Communications plays a critical role in facilitating an entire crisis response effort for both the public and private organizations. It is in an organization's interest to have a **crisis communications plan** to release verified information quickly. In doing so, it must express its empathy with any losses, ability to resolve the crisis and dedication to mitigate further damages.

In a perfect world, one spokesperson would serve as the sole source of information on an incident. In open societies, however, organizations in a crisis face the challenge of managing information while other channels can provide unanticipated and/or critical information affecting response operations. Art Botterell, Principal of the emergency information Internet company Incident.com and former staff member of the California Office of Emergency Services and the Federal Emergency Management Agency, validates this condition:

"Our emergency public information efforts have much more influence over operational outcomes than many of us likes to admit. Not only does news coverage inevitably feed back (hopefully not too much) into our command centers, [but] it also shapes the perspectives and expectations of responders and citizens alike."

Therefore, organizations must form a flexible and quickly activated Crisis Communications Team (CCT) to implement a communications plan as a part of their entire response effort.

Otherwise, the media will meet their story deadlines with or without the organization's input. By its very nature, the media abhor an information vacuum. It must be filled – if not by the organization, then by uninformed outsiders. Also, other involved entities will not conduct public relations for the organization.

Jane's Crisis Communications Handbook provides planning, response and post-incident procedures for organizations to communicate with their stakeholders and the media to inform, calm and direct the public during any crisis.

1.3 Consequences of inadequate communications
When an emergency occurs, crisis response teams (both government and private) tend to focus on mitigating the immediate effects of the incident.

Communications with stakeholders and the media is generally an afterthought. Any organization without a practiced response and communications plan will inevitably fail to coordinate messages among staff, with partners/authorities, to stakeholders and to the public via the media.

Also, reporters covering 'breaking news' often arrive on-site before, or soon after, the communications and/or entire response team. Without a quick response to the media, early press coverage, which often sets the tone for subsequent coverage, may be inaccurate or incomplete.

Preparation on all levels is vital for an effective communications response. For instance, if a receptionist fails to locate a spokesperson for a press inquiry, he or she could be responsible for a line in the next day's story stating, "A company spokesperson could not be reached for comment", suggesting secretiveness on the part of the organization.

The Oxford University study *The Impact of Catastrophes on Shareholder Value,* by Rory F Knight and Deborah J Pretty, concluded that corporations lost an average of 15 percent in net stock value in the months following an ineffective response to a large-scale emergency. Overall, message failures can lead to fatalities, casualties, lost elections, decreased funding, litigation, forfeited public/customer trust and/or property damage which could otherwise be prevented with a regularly rehearsed and updated crisis communications plan.

1.4 Benefits of effective crisis communications

A well-executed crisis communications response effort will increase an organization's credibility by:

◆ Providing vital information to stakeholders
◆ Displaying the organization's authority and capabilities
◆ Maintaining the organization's operations and mitigating losses
◆ Using the press cycle to aid response and recovery management

The Oxford University study found companies that managed a successful recovery gained an average of 5 percent in net stock value over the same time period as the ineffective corporations lost value. An effective response also increased companies' total market value by approximately 22 percent. The study asserts, "although all catastrophes have an initial negative impact on [company] value, paradoxically they offer an opportunity for management to demonstrate their talent in dealing with difficult circumstances." Furthermore, in the public eye, the positive impact of credible crisis response outweighs proof of financial well-being or recourse to those affected.

1.5 Changing security environment

The *Al-Qaeda* terrorist attacks in the United States on September 11, 2001 brought into sharp focus the need for organizations to prepare for widespread and sustained media attention. With little preparation, public and private CCT members and the media had to work closely together to disseminate calming and accurate information to the public.

The multi-layer response efforts included:

◆ Rescue and recovery missions in New York, Washington, DC and Pennsylvania
◆ New levels of security imposed in the United States
◆ Emergency closures and their impact on the US stock market, trade and travel flows, as well as the reverberations through the international economy
◆ Broadened international collaboration on counter-terror protection
◆ Cooperative international investigation of the attacks
◆ An international military campaign in Afghanistan

While these issues were still being assessed and addressed, the October 2001 anthrax threat to the US Postal Service, Congress and the media itself exacerbated the uncertainty and increased the media's response to any security-related news.

Media attention to these incidents also revealed response difficulties partly due to poor internal and external communication plans. For example, the US government did not have a unified internal broadcast system to evacuate government employees vulnerable to the terrorist attacks in the Washington, DC metropolitan area. The New York Police Department required several days to implement a cohesive communications action plan.

CNN National Correspondent Gary Tuchman recalls media access in New York soon after September 11:

> "I arrived in New York City around 3:00 in the morning, about 18 hours after the first plane struck the tower. Media access completely depended on which police officer you approached. If there was one message, it wasn't being communicated. Some officers would not let us drive on certain streets or go past barricades. Yet, we often found other officers who would. It is an uncomfortable position to have to shop for media-friendly officers, but the lack of organization and public need for information forced us to do so. As the days went by, the situation became very organized.
>
> For the most part, however, police did not allow the news media access to the Ground Zero site. Critical work was still taking place on the site, but allowing reporters access to such a huge area

would not have hampered that work or caused any
security problems. It also would have allowed our
viewing public to have more information in those
initial confusing and frightening days."

Although the scale of attacks on New York were beyond
any pre-incident plans, this experience reveals some
causes of a breakdown in orderly coverage, adversely
affecting the organization's message to the public:

◆   Failure to deliver a unified message and perimeter
    rules causes the media to go outside of the official
    CCT for site access and information
◆   Employees on-site act outside of the organization's
    command structure by independently serving as
    spokespersons in some capacity and managing
    perimeters/site access

Conversely, Lieutenant Colonel Robert Domenici, then
Commander of the US National Guard Weapons of
Mass Destruction Civil Response Unit in New York,
recalls the cooperation he experienced with the media
on September 11:

"The media was on hand in force and knew the
Civil Support Team was tied up in several sensitive
operations. The media wanted interviews and
information on operations. Because we had
trained with the media on hand prior to the incident
and conducted interviews in the past, they knew

our mission and the sensitivity of its nature. They worked out a time and place for interviews by holding meetings with the different sections. The media played a vastly different role by gathering this information and disseminating it back for the other sections to use in their operations. The media acted as a conduit and assistor in the information flow. Lesson learned: train with the media to ensure they know about your mission. Help them, [and] they will help you."

These examples show that ultimately, **both the organizations involved in a crisis and the media can, and in most cases want, to work together to inform the public.**

Another impact of September 11 on the media and security environment is that an incident occurring in one location can have a major impact on many other places. For instance, a terrorist attack on a ship in a port on the East coast of the United States will bring media scrutiny on organizations responsible for port security elsewhere in the US and around the world.

The new security environment makes it imperative to create, update and practice crisis communications plans with all employees before incidents occur. This planning will allow organizations to interact with media to calm the public while balancing the demands of operations and safety precautions.

1.6 Faster media cycle in response to crises

Two major dynamics have increased media response time to incidents. First, the current security environment demonstrates how the media can serve as a critical infrastructure and even 'first responder' to disseminate public safety information. Second, advances in information-based technology have significantly shortened media response time and increased access to different sources of information.

The continuing threat of multi-layer, safety-related crises have heightened press interest and public desire for calming, yet accurate messages. Consequently, **the media currently tend to infer that a security incident may be terrorism-related until it can be disproved.** For instance, when a suspected chemical-biological threat in Miami International Airport occurred on August 21, 2002, within five minutes of the response dispatch the local, national and international media sent a flurry of inquiries to the Miami-Dade Fire Rescue Public Affairs Office. Ultimately, the incident cause was not terrorism as speculated or even serious. (See *Chapter 3: Planning Procedures* for the full case study).

While the media now react more quickly to any news related to possible security threats, their limited resources and desire to report exclusives also shift their attention more quickly to the next big incident. In other words, the media target more resources to a particular story but for a shorter amount of time. For example, the TWA Flight 800 crash off the coast of New York in 1996 caused 230 fatalities and attracted over 600 members of the press for over 30 days. In contrast, the media coverage of American Airlines Flight 587 crash in Queens, New York on November 12, 2001 – that had more casualties, a similar potential terrorist cause and proximity to the same large media market – lasted for only about three days.

US Coast Guard Headquarters Station in Moriches, NY. Source: US Coast Guard   ***2002**/0535631*

Media presence around the US Coast Guard station to cover the 1996 TWA crash. Source: US Coast Guard ***2002****/0535632*

The expansion of the Internet, cable television and wireless communications facilitates quicker information access and delivery, creating a new media environment. For example, online searches provide a myriad of background information revealing organizations' past mistakes. This means that spokespersons must be more informed and prepared for probing questions. With this abundance of information, the media presents stories in a more condensed form, and therefore seeks striking quotes for 10- to 12-second sound bites. Some media organizations also combine elements of straight reporting and entertainment, whereby reporters may use controversy and sensationalism to increase ratings and therefore advertising revenue.

The new security environment and competitive pressures of the media industry heighten the need for organizations to form and test crisis response plans with a solid communications component.

1.7 Crisis cycle phases: response, communications and media

Most crises typically follow a similar sequence or structure. **Both short and long crisis response operations require a communications plan to be implemented simultaneously with other elements of the response.** The media in turn responds to these phases, requiring the CCT to inform them of developments. The following table details the phases of crises, communications and media response cycles and illustrates how they work in parallel.

Stage	Planning	Initial	Continuing	Diminishing	Resolution	Evaluation	Recognition
Operations	-Prepare response plans -Assess vulnerabilities -Train staff	-Treat injured -Assess scene -Establish perimeter	-Incident evolves/ contained -Resources allocated	-Response nears resolution -Resources reduced	-Crisis resolved -Resources reduced	-Response evaluated -Lessons learned -Institute improvements	-Convene anniversary/ memorial event
Communi-cations	-Establish a CCT -Develop media policies and procedures -Foster relationships with the press -Train staff -Equip a Crisis Center	-Activate CCT -Confirm facts -Assess situation -Identify stakeholders -Implement communications strategy -Develop external materials -Inform partners, stakeholders and media		-Re-assemble CCT -Confirm facts -Re-assess situation -Respond to stakeholders -Adjust messages/ strategy -Develop external materials -Inform partners, stakeholders and media	-Give response and crisis updates -Express gratitude for responders and community efforts	-Evaluate response -Compare lessons learned -Institute improvements	-Publicize the event -Send background material to media
Media*	-Develop contacts in public, private organizations -Create logistics response procedures -Train -Assign tasks	-Arrive on-scene -Require information and access -High level of local, national, international media attention -Coverage can be misleading/ conflicting	-Intense attention -Use expert commentary to fill information void -Coverage of people and/or groups may be inequitable	-Define nature of incident -Profile those involved in feature stories -Investigate incident cause and response	-Focus on causes, responsibilities, blame, efficacy of response/ recovery effort -Drop off in interest may occur	-Drop off in interest	-Spike in interest -Original or new reporters may cover the event -Focus on current status/ improvements

*Input from media scholar Dr. Christine M. Rodrigue, Professor at California State University

CHAPTER 1: Strategic Overview

1.8 Incident-based crisis communications

While every crisis communications response must involve executing the action plan, this handbook discusses a wide range of potential crises that attract varied types of media attention and require different internal and external communications responses.

◆ **Natural disasters:** sudden events, such as earthquakes, tornadoes, disease outbreaks or slower-moving events such as hurricanes and monsoons

◆ **Human-caused hazards:** unexpected, sometimes inexplicable human phenomena, such as (bio) terrorism, hoaxes, school or workplace violence, civil disturbances and armed conflict

◆ **Mechanical/technological malfunctions:** failures of public infrastructure or operations, such as transportation accidents, product failures and workplace facility emergencies

1.9 Public and private crisis communications

Depending on the level of the crisis, the incident may involve many spokespersons and communications mechanisms across the public and private sectors. Their legal obligations to release information, however, differ.

Government agencies have procedures usually guided by freedom of information policies in order to be accountable to the public. Desire for information may come in different forms: media inquiries, formal petitions for documents, letters of inquiry or phone calls to lawmakers and officials. Public agencies have stipulations on releasing certain types of information affecting operations, security, investigations and victims and their families. Most **public organizations also respond to emergencies using the Incident Command System (ICS)** to manage the incident with five functional areas: command (centralized location of management), operations, planning/intelligence, logistics, and finance and administration. The senior communications officer works in the command structure with the other incident command managers. In this handbook, that officer is referred to as the CCT Leader. In practice, the title varies from agency to agency. *Public agencies should clear all procedures adapted from this handbook with established ICS standard operating procedures.*

Private organizations, by contrast, can deem certain information proprietary and protect it from public scrutiny or discovery in legal actions. Private organizations, especially when they have investors, must be more circumspect about the information they make public, as this information may affect stock prices, financial standing or competition. Since private organizations do not have to follow mandated communications policies, they often do not have crisis communications procedures in place and greatly risk the consequences of an inadequate response.

When both types of organizations need to respond to the same incident, they must be aware of each other's information constraints. For example, Joint Information Centers (JIC) – mechanisms for organizations to coordinate and deliver their messages – are under the auspices of one lead organization, most likely a government entity responsible for managing the response operation.

Overall, public safety can depend on the ability of responders, CCTs and the media to inform, calm and listen to the public – the most critical infrastructure. Organizations therefore have a responsibility to plan and practice communications procedures to respond efficiently and quickly to emergencies.

CHAPTER 2: PRE-INCIDENT MEDIA RELATIONS

CHAPTER 2: PRE-INCIDENT MEDIA RELATIONS

2.1 Introduction

The news media serve as a critical infrastructure to report the facts of a crisis and communicate vital information to responders, stakeholders and the public. An organization's Crisis Communications Team (CCT) must prepare to engage with the media and understand how they operate in order to convey its message as effectively as possible. With 20 years of private and public emergency management experience, Bob Robinson, Managing Partner at the management firm Double R Consulting, emphasizes this need:

"What we [crisis responders] need to do is try and learn about how the media really works so we can figure out how to make them a positive information transmitting resource...we need to focus on the media as a resource challenge, and not take up space yapping about political unfairness or biases."

In turn, this chapter will discuss the following aspects of understanding media operations and implementing pre-incident media relations procedures:

◆ Role of the media during emergencies
◆ Fostering relationships with the media
◆ Influences on media coverage
◆ Types of media organizations

◆   Journalistic ethics
◆   Creating media pool procedures

2.2 Role of the media during emergencies

The media are an organization's link to the public before, during and after a crisis. Because citizens receive the majority of their information through the press, the media also influences public perception on all areas of society on local, national and global levels. Therefore, **the CCT and the press should develop relationships before a crisis occurs and work as partners** rather than adversaries, especially during emergencies.

Media role in hurricane warnings

The Miami, Florida office of the National Hurricane Center and the reporters who cover it illustrate the symbiotic relationship between responders and the media during a crisis. When a hurricane threatens the region, meteorologists at the Center develop forecasts and issue warnings. The media, in turn, transmit this information to the public, along with interpretive commentary.

Max Mayfield, the Center's director, is respected by the media for his efforts to release information promptly. He, in turn, appreciates the media's role. He does not expect favorable coverage at all times, but in a crisis, he says, "We can't get our message to the public without them, and that makes them a big player on the team."

Organizations responding to a crisis must accept that **the media will always report a story based on the information available, whether or not the CCT supplies or verifies the information.**

2.2.1 Reporting phases

While individual reporters use different styles, the 'inverted pyramid' serves as a story development formula, especially for print media. Using this formula, the most important developments and details are stated in the beginning of the story and the least important material at the bottom, where it can be trimmed, if necessary, because of space limitations. In the course of a crisis life cycle, news coverage generally goes through the following stages:

Initial
◆ Reporters, editors and producers rush to the scene to catch up with the story and to report basic facts: who, what, when and where. The 'why' usually comes later.
◆ Stories usually do not require much investigative reporting, creative input or editorial meetings

Continuing
◆ The initial, breaking-news stage is over, and the crisis may have taken a new turn. For instance, the hurricane has passed but food and water are now in short supply.

Diminishing

◆ Story ideas come from reporters/producers on the ground. For example, a reporter might do a profile story on one of the crisis response workers.

Diminishing/resolution

◆ Follow-on stories usually (but not always) take an analytical perspective:
  • Why did this happen?
  • What does it mean?
  • Who is to blame?
  • What could have been done differently?
  • What new, preventive measures are now being taken?

Recognition

◆ Stories cover expected anniversaries and/or commemorative events
◆ These stories focus on the background of the incident, recovery and current state of operations, including improvements or continued failures. (Many times, new reporters cover these events as the original reporters have moved to other jobs or are not assigned to the story.)

The uncertainty of the initial phase of a crisis presents the greatest challenge not only for responders but also for the media. By way of example, the British Broadcasting Corporation (BBC) Newsgathering

---

department is a small team of assignment editors who work in shifts around the clock to oversee daily national news coverage for network television, radio and the Internet. The competition in those three markets creates the need for rapid response to developing stories. John Curran, BBC Home Assignment Editor in the Newsgathering department, describes the intensity of an initial media deployment:

> "When we get a major breaking news event in those crucial early hours it's not about issues or in depth analysis or shiny graphics or studio pundits, it's about one thing: logistics. We call it 'arses on aeroplanes.' We serve seven radio networks and five television channels. That means we have to adopt the attitude and tactics, 'there firstest with the mostest.'"

2.3 Fostering relationships with the media
Developing good relationships with the media is an ongoing responsibility of the CCT. The process must begin before a crisis occurs and maintained subsequently. Building good professional relationships with the media takes time, but it can pay dividends in ensuring accurate reporting of an organization's regular operations and response to a crisis.

Cooperating for accuracy

A reporter was going to run a story on the US Air Force he believed to be true. The reporter had researched the topic and wanted to print a factual story. When he called to ask a question, the Public Affairs Director Captain Joseph Della Vedova learned the angle of the story and realized it was missing some key facts that would change the direction of the article. Because Captain Della Vedova had already formed a relationship with the reporter, he was able to work with the reporter to fill in the details. The result was a balanced and factual news article.

Source: Captain Joseph Della Vedova, Public Affairs Director, US Air Force

The CCT Leader–reporter relationship is vital to smooth communications before, during and after incidents. (See *Chapter 3: Planning Procedures* for more information on the role and characteristics and of the CCT Leader.) The CCT members should research and acquaint themselves with the reporters, editors and producers who cover their industry or area. Even though the reporters are the ones speaking on camera or conducting interviews, **producers and editors often act as the key players in deciding on coverage and story angles.** It is just as important to develop relationships with them as with the reporters.

John Curran, BBC Home Assignment Editor, emphasizes the influence of editors on site:

> "The cast iron rule is 'be there.' You cannot run a major incident or news event from a warm office with hot food and nearby toilets. You need to get out to the scene. Be there and be seen to be there. Walk the plot. You can then spot problems and tackle them before they get out of hand. We deploy an assignment editor or news organizer to be ringmaster for the BBC circus – they are also the person who follows the elephants with a shovel."

To develop and nurture a relationship with members of the media, use the following strategies:

Information on the press
◆ **Media contact list:** research the names of reporters, editors and producers who cover, or are likely to cover, the organization. Obtain as much contact information as possible, including **cell phone, office phone, fax numbers and e-mail addresses.**
◆ **Media types:** research all relevant radio, print, and broadcast media sources. Include the local, national and international affiliates as well as trade publications.
◆ **Regularly update the contact list:** Media staff tend to move frequently. Even if they stay in the

same company, they will most likely change jobs on a regular basis.

Proactive engagement with the press

◆ **Coverage response:** follow up on any news story about the organization by contacting the principal reporter. Share the organization's thoughts about the story and offer to provide assistance in the future.

◆ **Regular contact:** periodically contact journalists who have written about the organization as well as others who cover the organization/industry. Even a one-minute conversation can communicate the CCT's accessibility and interest in working with the press.

◆ **Visits to media organizations:** periodic, brief visits to news organizations can be an effective way for reporters and CCT members to keep current with each other's concerns and timetables

◆ **New product/facility:** invite the media to any roll-out or opening of a new, large-scale product or infrastructure expansion. For example, when branches of the US military purchase or launch a significant new technological capability, it gives members of the press a tour of its facilities to inform them of the benefits.

◆ **Training exercises:** invite the media to training exercises, especially if the organization routinely deals with public safety situations. Reporters, editors and producers do seek to educate themselves on the technicalities of their beat. Training exercises are a good way for them to 'quick train' as well as to develop relationships with the organization.

◆ **Media guide:** distribute information on the specific responsibilities of the CCT Leader, policy makers within the organization and the chain of command (including CCT backup). This can be an annual publication or simply a faxed announcement, depending on the size of the organization. During a crisis, the guide can expedite a reporter's search for official word on rumored developments.

◆ **CCT Leader access:** the CCT Leader should give out contact information to make him/herself available to the media to provide or verify information. Ready access displays to the media that the organization is the first source for accurate information and timely comment.

Taking these steps is vitally important because the organization is not the only source for a reporter. **During crisis, the organization will compete with other organizations, commentators and other breaking news stories to convey their message through the media.**

2.3.1 Response to media interest
The key to maintaining a good relationship with media representatives is to respond to their queries within their time constraints. The CCT Leader must **respect equal**

access for all members of the press, **but should not publicize in advance that one reporter is about to run a certain story.** Of course, neither party should use friendships to comprise professional integrity. Maintaining equal access also does not mean ignoring differences in reporter behavior. **When one reporter violates established ground rules**, such as going beyond a perimeter or interviewing children involved in the incident, **the CCT should not penalize the entire press corps.** This will only create friction between the media and the organization.

Keep the following guidelines in mind:

Interviews
◆ Make officials available for one-on-one interviews, or, at the very least, for round-table discussions or media briefings
◆ Keep scheduled interview appointments. Understand that reporters invest considerable time in preparing for interviews and that they depend on timely interviews to meet their deadlines.
◆ If an interview is not possible, provide written responses to questions by the reporter's deadline
◆ Do not wait until the deadline to tell a reporter that an interview will not be possible or a written response is not ready
◆ Keep reporters apprised of the status of their queries

Source: Michael C Sirak, Staff Reporter, Jane's Defence Weekly

Media and law enforcement: the sniper shootings

The 'sniper' shootings in the Washington, DC area in October 2002 attracted massive public and media attention. Press coverage also focused on the police-media relations. For example, incident commander, Montgomery County Police Chief Charles Moose, chastised the media for reporting a tarot 'death' card found at the site of the eighth shooting had a note on it reading, "Dear Policeman, I am God."

Although a law enforcement source had leaked the information, he said, "there is no room, in my mind, for both" the media and the police to solve the case. Nevertheless, the media broadcast of a suspected car license plate number and color helped a witness identify the car of two key suspects the police later arrested.

Lessons learned: treat the media as a partner, not an adversary. Do not blame the press for leaks. Instead, focus on tighter internal policies and explain to the press how using information unofficially announced may hinder the investigation. Hold press conferences for only milestone events. Chief Moose held up to five conferences per day without announcing major developments. This contributed to outside speculation increasing, instead of calming public fears.

Information distribution

◆ Have a means to distribute film footage (also known

as b-roll), photos and illustrations electronically via
the Internet
◆ Make available for distribution, if at all possible, any
new or timely documents referenced at press
briefings or during interviews

2.4 Influences on media coverage

It is important to understand that the media have
different priorities than those of an organization the
crisis affects. To be competitive, reporters attempt to
gather information sooner and in more detail than their
rivals. Though reporters do not fixate on business
concerns, the majority of media outlets are for-profit
organizations and their commercial success depends
on beating competitors to stories. Providing exclusive
information increases readership, thus advertising and
revenue.

Whether a story is deemed newsworthy often depends
on the presence, or absence, of other significant news.
For example, on a 'slow news day' a workplace-violence
incident may attract national coverage, whereas on a
busier news day only local media outlets would cover
the incident.

The angle a particular media outlet takes on a story can
depend on a variety of factors:

◆ **Current news environment:** the main themes
being reflected in the media will affect story

selection and depth of coverage. Media outlets influence one another. If a crisis story breaks in the print media, other press organizations will follow-up on the incident and vice versa. Television and radio producers/editors read newspapers to sketch the outlines of their own programming. Print editors monitor television and radio to find out what they may have missed.

Influence of media focus

In the summer of 2001, daily news coverage focused on a series of shark attacks off American beaches. The events of September 11, however, immediately turned media attention to terrorism and the fight against it. In this changed environment, certain incidents (such as a gas explosion in New York City) that were initially thought to be terrorist-related received widespread coverage. Before 9/11 they most likely would have received minimal attention.

◆ **Reporter/editor/producer experience:** the experience and expertise that a reporter, editor or producer brings to a story will influence the angle, including the analysis and details emphasized

◆ **Target market or audience:** identifying the audience of a media outlet before providing information or answering questions will help organizations deliver information tailored to the focus of that outlet. For example, in the event of a hurricane, a local television station will need to know about road, school, and business closings, while an international television news channel will be interested in large-scale weather patterns and effects on air travel and commercial trade.

◆ **Ownership and/or political affiliation:** the CCT should be aware of possible political affiliations before an incident takes place, so they can respond appropriately to the demands of competing – and sometimes adversarial – media agencies. For example, a trade union newspaper will probably cover a workplace shooting differently than an industry association magazine.

Though basic, these points are easily forgotten during a crisis. It is therefore essential that the CCT establish constructive working relationships with the media and gain an appreciation of their needs before an incident occurs. This will help the CCT develop crisis communications plans that meet the media requirements *and* communicate the organization's key messages.

2.4.1 Newsworthy events
Several types of crises generally attract media attention:

◆ Incidents affecting many people, especially locally but also on national and/or international levels:
  • Major public safety incidents
  • Terrorism
  • Mass casualties

- • War or large-scale conflict
- • Violence involving children
- • Natural disasters
- ◆ Incompetence or wrongdoing on the part of a government agency or a corporation
- ◆ Dangerous commercial products
- ◆ Incidents of public outrage and civil disturbance
- ◆ Criminal investigations or trials with significant legal or social impact
- ◆ Local stories that affect others outside the community
- ◆ Events that yield unexpected, shocking, bizarre, exotic details and/or images
- ◆ Human interest stories (such as the rescue of a small child or animal)
- ◆ Stories with celebrity involvement
- ◆ Stories deemed to be of public interest by news editors

2.5 Types of media organizations

Understanding the scheduling requirements of different media outlets helps the CCT respond to varying deadlines most effectively. Media outlets can use different formats, thus manage and create stories on different timeframes. In hour-by-hour dealings with the media, the CCT should respond to television, radio and online queries first and then daily and weekly newsprint queries later that day.

See the following table to review these differing requirements.

Type	Format	Needs	Lead Time
Online	Electronic, web-conference, chats, bulletin boards	Quotes, facts, leads, photos, graphics, video	Immediate, days or weeks for scheduled expert participation
Television	24-hour, news hour, talk show, (live/taped)	Video footage (b-roll), site access, slides of logo/product, sound bites	Immediate, hours, days or weeks
Radio	24-hour, news hour, talk show (live/taped)	Sound bites, interviews (phone, in-studio, on-site)	Immediate, hours, days or weeks
Newspaper	Daily, weekly	Quotes, facts, leads, photos, graphics, interviews	Immediate, hours for breaking story, days, weeks for features
Trade magazine	Weekly, monthly	Quotes, facts, industry or government reports, product or personnel photos	Days, weeks, months; features linked to planned or expected events
General-interest magazine	Weekly, monthly	Quotes, facts, leads, photos, graphics	Weeks or months

Source: Derived from The Making of a Corporate Spokesperson—Media Interview Technique, The Loeb Group, 1999

2.5.1 Internet

The Internet is often the first place people go to for information on an unfolding incident. Internet media outlets function much like 24-hour broadcast news channels. Established media maintain regularly updated websites on the Internet and new online-only media organizations have also sprung up. Consequently, international coverage from a wide range of perspectives is as easily available as local coverage.

Internet sites offer readers options beyond those of the traditional media:

◆ Interactivity ('web casts' with guest experts, chat rooms, bulletin boards for reader responses)
◆ Updated incident timelines
◆ Archived articles, footage, voice interviews
◆ 'Links' to other organizations for more specific information
◆ Various post-incident resources, for instance, services for readers who want to make charitable donations, file insurance claims, obtain unemployment assistance, receive psychological counseling or arrange for funeral/memorial services

The Internet can spread information – and misinformation – very quickly. **Rumors can now spin out of control** and gain global attention in a matter of minutes or hours via the website or by users forwarding articles to others by e-mail. Moreover, **Internet news sites are under competitive pressure to post first and fact checking and copy editing may not always be stringently practiced.**

2.5.2 Television
During an emergency, television stations will broadcast updates as the situation evolves. The assignment desk may learn of the event from weather satellite images, emergency response radio dispatches or other media sources. National and international stations may respond to an event based on local coverage.

Role of producers and editors
The producer at the assignment desk sends a producer, a reporter or both, along with a camera crew to the incident to start covering the event on-air as soon as possible. For at least the first few hours, this team will operate on an ad hoc basis as they obtain additional information and/or circumstances change. Most likely, the team will work from the site designated for the press, and will have broadcast vans and any other vehicles used to obtain nearby access, such as helicopters, cherry pickers and boats.

Spokespeople need to be aware that editing can completely change the meaning of a statement longer than a 10 to 12 second sound bite. If a mistake occurs in the editing process, it is often too late to repair the damage because the correction will be very short and most likely broadcasted to a different audience. See section *6.4 Key messages* to develop concise sound bites.

'Non-breaking' feature stories are developed in a more deliberate process. This involves identifying a story idea, locating sources, clearing the concept with editors and producers and placing the piece on an appropriate program. Some stories are immediately approved, others are thoroughly discussed and many are rejected. Even on 24-hour news networks, space for features is limited.

Sources: Laura Powell, Media Consultant, Laura Powell Productions; Gary Tuchman, National Correspondent, CNN

2.5.3 Radio
During breaking news, radio reporters are for the most part on their own with the tape recorder on hand. In many cases, their immediate challenge is to reach the location where news is breaking. To provide live, on-scene coverage, reporters need access to the site and to broadcast from the radio station's van. The vehicle's communications resources also provide additional incident information beyond the physical reporting site. Sound bites are as important for radio as for television. They are slightly longer, due to the audio format and should range from 10 to 20 seconds, ideally. **Radio reporters seek captivating, clear, concise and newsworthy sound bites.**

Role of producers and editors

The on-site reporter is central to coverage but producers and editors also play important roles. Radio producers on location are central to making story decisions and providing reporter support including:

◆ Framing coverage as events unfold
◆ Setting coverage priorities
◆ Arranging transportation and other technical and logistical support
◆ Providing the reporter updates from other sources to help identify spokespersons and interview subjects

The radio editor manages the 'big picture' by setting the agenda for regular programs, feature programs and interviews. These elements are regularly discussed in daily staff meetings. Their tactical responsibilities include:

◆ Assigning reporters to stories
◆ Prioritizing coverage and determining story length
◆ Deciding when to break into regular programming with 'flash' coverage of breaking events

In-depth stories or interviews focus on a particular aspect or angle **of the crisis at hand**. Plans and schedules for detailed background, historical and analytical stories are usually decided well in advance of airing.

Covering large scale events

On September 11, 2001, a major priority and challenge for a radio reporter in Washington, DC was to be as close to the Pentagon as possible to report what was happening on the scene. At the same time, however, many other aspects of the event, such as people evacuating the city, traffic jams, confusion, panic and heroic acts, served as news used later on different programs. This shows how organizations responding to large scale events choose to report angles and information secondary to the actual incident.

Source: Drora Perl, Washington Bureau Chief, Galei-Tzahal (Tel-Aviv Radio)

2.5.4 Daily newspapers

Daily newspapers often provide background beyond what broadcast news reports. Reporters have individual styles and methods for writing an article and may choose a technique based on the specific incident. Complex stories might require an outline; simple stories might not. The best reporters tend to be the fastest writers. They mentally prepare their articles from the moment they reach the scene – and in some cases, even before arriving. First impressions can be critical. **If the CCT does not appear to be in command of the facts, the team may not be able to recapture the interest and respect of the media or counter incorrect preconceptions.**

The hardest part of any story to write is the lead – the very beginning of the story – where the writer tries to 'hook' the reader. For most writers, once the lead is under control, the rest of the story flows naturally. The best writers quickly find a working lead and then refine it as the day unfolds, sometimes in consultation with the editor. **A spokesperson's statements often suggest angles, or the emphasis/direction of a story, to members of the media.** As the CCT frames the key messages and spokesperson comments, be aware that different reporters may perceive the comments differently, thus creating different angles, or versions of the incident.

Role of editors

A newspaper editor assigns reporters to cover specific incidents and may work with them on developing an angle. An editor also takes control over the article once a reporter files the story. Most editors consult with the writer during this process and the best writers insist that this consultation take place. The story then goes to a different set of editors who decide:

◆ Location of the article in the newspaper
◆ Length of the piece
◆ Which editor writes the headline

Few newspaper reporters write the headline to their articles. Furthermore, the reporter rarely has any input in, or control of, the headline. Headline writing is a difficult art, as the headline writer must capture the essence of a long, complex story to draw the readers' attention. Headlines state the most noteworthy, and often controversial, aspect of a story. If the organization does not like a headline, discuss it with the reporter but never blame the reporter. Do not expect the reporter to address the headline complaint. Only contact the editor to complain about a headline if it is truly incorrect.

2.5.5 Weekly magazines

Weekly magazines strive to go beyond the basic 'who, what, where, when and why,' adding detail and analysis. Articles need to provide exclusive coverage of a subject, or at least offer a fresh perspective on topics that the daily newspapers and competing magazines have already reported. **Weekly magazines also have more time to verify and obtain information.**

Specialty magazines, such as industry or trade publications, have a targeted audience and rely on comments and input from policymakers typically inside government and industry. General news magazines have more freedom to use outside analysts.

For both types of magazines, CCT cooperation in providing access to officials, or information from them, is critical to the success of weekly magazine articles. If cooperation is not forthcoming, reporters have no choice but to bypass official channels and contact the officials directly or to use commentary from individuals who lack complete information and/or have competing interests to the affected organization. This is especially true for breaking events.

Role of editors

Each week, a magazine's chief editor holds a staff meeting to determine the focus of the magazine's next issue. The editor provides an overall direction and highlights topics of interest. The reporters provide feedback and insights based on their own interviews, research and on developments in the news. Story development starts with the editor's decision to:

◆ Assign a story to the reporter
◆ Approve the reporter's story suggestion
◆ Assess the reporter's story angle

Based on this exchange, the editor and reporters assemble a story list for the week.

The editors responsible for the different sections of the magazine have a set number of pages to fill each week. Filling the pages is a dynamic process. A major story may break in mid-week, forcing the editor to reprioritize reporters' efforts. A story may unfold more slowly than anticipated or an exclusive story may develop more quickly than expected. If deviations in the story list arise, the reporters inform the editor.

Source: Michael C Sirak, Staff Reporter, Jane's Defence Weekly

2.5.6 Differences in coverage

Overall, the coverage of a specific media outlet depends on its delivery medium and target market. Different outlets covering the same incident will require very different information on different time scales. Each will place different demands on the organizations involved in the response effort.

For example, a hurricane could be covered very differently in the following media outlets:

◆ **24-hour TV news channel:** will require instant and continuous information (including images) on casualties and damage, the emergency services response (who, how many, where from, rescue efforts and so on), quotes from local and possibly national leaders as well as interviews with the affected population (the 'human interest' element)

◆ **Weekly insurance industry trade magazine:** will focus on the property damage and the impact on the industry, the companies affected, the size of likely insurance payouts, quotes from insurance sector executives and so on

◆ **Monthly lifestyle magazine:** likely to focus on the human consequences of the incident, with in-depth interviews of those most affected – both victims and emergency service personnel. It will also require background information on previous hurricanes and how the response differed in this incident.

◆ **Internet-only environmental news site:** will

require information on the environmental impact of the hurricane with special attention given to any local endangered species, flora and fauna. Its bulletin board of reader response can serve as a source of public feedback.

2.6 Journalistic ethics

The vast majority of the media make every effort to perform their duties ethically and with a sense of fairness. Understanding the press's commitment to their profession can assist the CCT in understanding the parameters of what the media has a right to report. Conversely, **these guidelines give insight in establishing ground rules and deciding if a correction is justified.**

The Society of Professional Journalists (SPJ) is a broad-based journalism organization with 9,000 members in the United States. It has adopted an extensive and detailed Code of Ethics for its members and the profession at large. According to the SPJ, the code, "instructs journalists to seek truth and report it, minimize harm, act independently and be accountable." Within this framework, SPJ outlines the following best practices for its members to abide:

◆   Test the accuracy of information from all sources and exercise care to avoid inadvertent error. Deliberate distortion is never permissible.
◆   Diligently seek out subjects of news stories to give

them the opportunity to respond to allegations of wrongdoing

◆ Make certain that headlines, news teases and promotional material, photos, video, audio, graphics, sound bites and quotations do not misrepresent. They should not oversimplify or highlight incidents out of context.

◆ Never distort the content of news photos or video

◆ Image enhancement for technical clarity is always permissible

◆ Always label montages and photo illustrations

◆ Recognize a special obligation to ensure that the public's business is conducted in the open and that government records are open to inspection

◆ Show compassion for those who may be affected adversely by news coverage

◆ Use special sensitivity when dealing with children and inexperienced sources or subjects

◆ Be sensitive when seeking or using interviews or photographs of those affected by tragedy or grief

◆ Recognize that gathering and reporting information may cause harm or discomfort

◆ Pursuit of the news is not a license for arrogance

◆ Clarify and explain news coverage and invite dialogue with the public over journalistic conduct

◆ Encourage the public to voice grievances against the news media

◆ Admit mistakes and correct them promptly

More information from the Society of Professional

Journalists (SPJ) can be found at: http://www.spj.org/ethics_code.asp.

For a list of European ethics sites, see: Ethic Net: Databank for European Codes of Journalism Ethic at: www.uta.fi/ethicnet/.

Michigan State University *School of Journalism* established the *Victims and the Media Program* to promote appropriate coverage of victims of violence and catastrophe. Its expanding program goals include:

◆ Instruct journalism students and working reporters in covering and interviewing victims with sensitivity
◆ Support working reporters in dealing with the stresses and trauma of crisis reporting
◆ Assist victim advocates and service providers in dealing with their roles as facilitators and buffers between victims and the media

More information on the program and links to related media and service provider resources can be found at http://victims.jrn.msu.edu/.

2.7 Creating a media pool

A media pool consists of one or more members of the press who agree to be the sole video/photographic and/or reporting representatives for the entire news media covering the incident. Use pools when security and safety concerns exist, or if a large media presence

Pool coverage of hurricanes

Bob Sheets, Director of the National Hurricane Center (NHC), and the press corps who cover NHC operations together created a formal pool agreement. They determined which outlets would provide staff and equipment.

They also set up a rotation of four-minute interview 'windows' throughout the day, giving each pool member exclusive access to NHC staff for a one-on-one interview. The rotation, which sometimes produces as many as 80 short interviews per day, also allows flexible interview times based on unique deadline requirements. Priority for access is given to outlets serving the area the hurricane threatens.

The timing of the agreement catalyzed the media to participate in the planning, purchase and installation of about US$100,000 in equipment in NHC's new facility. Cables are thus no longer spread through the operational areas.

In the inevitable presence of conflicting information from the media, the public may delay action until they detect a consensus in the information. The NHC pool serves as both original source and a standard by which all other reports may be judged.

Source: Frank Lepore, Public Affairs Officer, NHC

could be disruptive – for example, during an incident involving violence towards children. Media organizations are not fond of pooling, but it is established practice in certain contexts, such as military campaigns and of the activities of heads of state.

Using an internal videographer/photographer
Another option for managing a pool is to have someone from the response organization(s) trained as a videographer/photographer provide still or video imagery. This is effective only when the organization has established its credibility for accurate information, so that media feel comfortable with the individual documenting the incident.

Procedures
Regardless of who is collecting the imagery, the CCT Leader must accompany the videographer/ photographer to ensure his/her safety and that footage does not violate any laws or privacy/confidentiality requirements.

The following planning procedures can help an organization manage media pools effectively:

◆ If possible, set up interview access time windows, and assign a media representative for one-on-one interviews and/or video access

◆ Prioritize media access to outlets serving areas the crisis threatens the most – for instance, during natural disasters

◆ If space for travel or accommodation is limited, let the media decide which organizations participate. For example, when rafters from Cuba floated a hundred miles off the coast of Florida, the US Coast Guard gave the media 30 minutes to decide which four reporters out of 100 would ride on a helicopter for an over flight.

◆ When dealing with a regular press corps, consider asking them for funds to purchase and use custom equipment. This will minimize space needed for video gear and cabling and will ensure high-quality footage for everyone.

◆ Conduct media training and familiarization exercises on 'what to expect and how to be prepared.' Remember, if there is a vital story to tell, the media will reach the crisis area one way or another.

◆ Establish a rapport with the media videographers and photographers and understand their needs

◆ When participating in a Joint Information Center (JIC) and managing a pool, recognize jurisdictional boundaries. A JIC is a mechanism for multiple organizations to collaborate on implementing a communications plan. See section *3.7 Cooperation with other organizations* to establish relationships with potential JIC organizations and section *6.3 Creating a Joint Information Center (JIC)* to implement a JIC plan.

◆ Inform the media of the travel timetable, as well as any supplies and accommodation they will need to arrange for themselves

Deploying with the press

The Miami-Dade Florida Urban Search and Rescue Task Force has been deployed to disasters around the world. Response organizers have tried to accommodate reporters' requests to join deployments. The goal has been to show the public first-hand what the task force was doing overseas in challenging environments. However, problems that arose included:

◆ Some members of the media were untrained and lacked passports, necessary supplies and equipment, thus risked delaying the deployment

◆ Logistics for the media were difficult as pre-packed equipment caches and portable housing were for task force members only and aircraft space was limited

◆ The participating organizations did not have a consensus on the level of prioritizing media involvement

The need to respond quickly and effectively in a crisis often limits the potential for positive media coverage. These difficulties can be reduced through planning and education of the media pool.

CHAPTER 3: PLANNING PROCEDURES

CHAPTER 3: PLANNING PROCEDURES

3.1 Planning for a crisis response
While no one can predict a crisis, every organization can and should identify its vulnerabilities. Preparations for a possible crisis should include forming a Crisis Communications Team (CCT) to implement the communications part of the response plan. These measures give an organization the best possible chance of engaging fellow responders, stakeholders and the public during any crisis quickly and effectively.

3.2 Create a Crisis Communications Team
An organization should designate a small group of people who have the authority to make and implement decisions and the training to act as spokespersons. The CCT should include senior-level representatives from:

- Senior leadership, including senior or deputy directors
- Corporate communications/public affairs
- Legal affairs
- Human resources
- Investor relations
- Government relations, community affairs
- Security and/or risk management
- Information technology
- Operations management

The team may also include consultants, used on an ongoing basis, for areas such as communications, legal affairs and security.

Finally, the CCT should have support staff to perform the following functions:

◆ Media queries/media log maintenance
◆ Media monitoring
◆ Research
◆ Editing/writing
◆ Website updates
◆ Equipping and maintaining a Crisis Center and press conference area

Crises that threaten an organization and/or a community are often of concern to many different stakeholders with diverse or even conflicting information needs. During the **initial phase** of a crisis, information coming from on-scene personnel and the media is usually incomplete. Therefore, if information-gathering and communications response procedures are not already in place, confusion will impede the entire response process.

3.3 Crisis Communications Team Leader
An organization needs one point of contact to build a consensus on its communications strategy and to articulate its crisis response strategy. Additionally, the CCT needs someone to prepare, implement and

evaluate a communications strategy or standard operations procedures. The CCT Leader usually manages these functions.

3.3.1 Role of a Crisis Communications Team Leader

During an incident, the CCT Leader must communicate with internal management while meeting the information needs of the public and key stakeholders. The CCT Leader is responsible for these core duties:

Internal

◆ Assembling the CCT
◆ Arranging strategy meetings or conference calls
◆ Briefing senior management on the CCT strategy and actions
◆ If necessary, briefing specific departments or the entire staff of an organization on the CCT strategy and actions
◆ Training staff on media relations: interviews, press conferences, press queries
◆ Informing the staff of ongoing developments and of changing organizational positions on an incident
◆ Tracking media and stakeholder responses to communications activity
◆ Evaluating the overall communications response to an incident
◆ Coordinating third-party spokespeople

External

◆ Fostering relationships with the media before, during and after an event
◆ Representing the organization to the public, the press and key stakeholders
◆ Serving as the main point of contact for external queries, especially from the media
◆ Acting as the primary spokesperson
◆ Sourcing all handout material, such as background video, fact sheets, talking points, staff biographies and so on

In government agencies, the CCT Leader is often the Public Information Officer (PIO) or Public Affairs Officer (PAO). In private organizations, the CCT Leader is often the Public Relations (PR) manager or a corporate communications manager or another communications staff member. Many organizations, however, do not have a dedicated staff member due to budget or staff limitations or a perceived lack of need.

In the public sector, the spokesperson may be a volunteer or assigned to the job. Either way, the person should have a desire to be in that position. Before selecting an individual to fill the role, an organization should identify internal needs and priorities:

◆ What are the organization's communications objectives?

- Does the communications strategy require a full- or part-time commitment?
- How large is the media market surrounding the organization, and will it require a large or a small communications staff?
- How much will the CCT staff requirements increase during a crisis?

3.3.2 Characteristics of a Crisis Communications Team Leader

The following skill set represents the qualities of an effective CCT Leader:

Internal management

- Possesses thorough working knowledge of the organization and sector/industry
- Has credibility within the organization, and will not hesitate to tell leaders what to say publicly during a crisis
- Understands that senior officials act as spokespersons for milestone events only. (Senior officials should be close to the response effort as much as possible.)
- Understands senior management goals to increase the organization's effectiveness through public understanding and support
- Listens closely
- Quick to follow-up on queries
- Possesses or can manage a staff with multilingual capabilities

External relations

◆ Speaks to the public and on camera comfortably and with aplomb regarding 'routine' crisis issues:
  • Media ground rules, briefing schedules
  • Information verification
  • Basic incident response and recovery questions: who, what, where, when, why
  • Establishment of toll-free numbers for further information and/or feedback
◆ Fits the organization's desired image
◆ Writes and edits clearly and quickly
◆ Understands how the media operate, including their access and technology needs
◆ Knows how to build relationships with reporters, editors and producers
◆ Listens closely
◆ Quick to follow-up on queries
◆ Well groomed, professional appearance

Overall, a CCT Leader must **be able to multitask operationally and also to balance the internal and external demands for information.** If he or she does not understand the nature of internal management and operations, the CCT Leader will not be a credible representative of the organization.

Within an organization, it may be hard to find someone with all these characteristics who is not already fulfilling the communications role. Many of the skills, however, can be acquired through training. Some training may come through public speaking, media relations or journalism courses. Learning about all of the areas of operations can also provide a good deal of training.

Overall, the CCT Leader **must be able to promote a consistent message, exhibit empathy, answer questions knowledgeably and honestly** and **follow-through** after an incident.

Establishing credibility

During the October 2001 anthrax letter attacks in the United States, an officer of the Epidemic Intelligence Service (EIS) of the Centers for Disease Control and Prevention (CDC) met with workers from the Brentwood postal facility in Washington, DC, where two employees died of anthrax exposure. The EIS officer was describing appropriate medical prevention methods to the workers when an activist in the crowd began to shout inflammatory comments. Because the EIS officer had established himself as a credible and trusted source of information, the crowd told the activist to be quiet so they could hear what the EIS officer had to say.

Source: CDC Crisis and Emergency Risk Communication, September 2002

3.4 Communications planning procedures

The Team Leader, in coordination with the CCT, should create policies and procedures that give clear guidelines for communicating with the press and key

---

stakeholders. In doing so, **all staff should operate from the same set of information during a crisis in order to convey a consistent message.** Outline these policies in an internal document and include input from legal and other departments to ensure compliance with appropriate laws, regulations and the crisis response policies.

Communications policies and procedures should:

◆ State the goals and the objectives of the media policy
◆ Demonstrate the organization's highest authority approved the policy
◆ Identify the responsibilities of the CCT within the organization and its overall crisis response structure
◆ Provide all contact details for the CCT: work/home/cell/fax phone numbers and e-mail addresses
◆ List the steps mandated when a crisis occurs or when members of the press or key stakeholders approach the organization. Write and distribute a script for dealing with these questions.
  • The CCT implementation of the communications component of the crisis response plan involves **seven steps**:
    (1) Activate the CCT
    (2) Gather and verify information
    (3) Assess the gravity of the crisis
    (4) Identify key stakeholders
    (5) Implement a communications strategy

(6) Develop external materials
(7) Inform partners, stakeholders and media

See the following chapters for guidance on each component of the **seven-step response plan**:

- *Chapter 5: Gathering and Verifying Information*
- *Chapter 6: Messages and Strategy*
- *Chapter 7: Engaging Key Stakeholders*
- *Chapter 8: Working with the Media*

The CCT should craft a cover memorandum to these policies explaining the organization's vision for an effective communications plan. The head of the organization and the CCT should sign this memo to reinforce senior-level commitment to crisis communications preparedness. See the following example letter.

MEMORANDUM
TO: All employees
FROM: Highest ranking staff member and CCT
RE: Media Policy

[Organization name] is committed to sharing its assurances of [customer, public] service through [state organization's mission].

In the event we confront an emergency, [CCT leader] will manage our Crisis Communications Team, including [list team names]. Using the attached procedures they have created, we will have preparations in place to provide timely information as a part of our larger crisis management process.

At all times, employees and management should refer reporters to the CCT for any information they may need. This will ensure that our organization communicates clearly, while avoiding potentially inaccurate or conflicting reports. Employees should *only* participate in media interviews with authorization from [CCT Leader].

If reporters approach you directly, your response should be:

"Thank you for your interest in our organization but our policy is to have [name of CCT department] respond to all media inquires. Please give me your name and number and I'll have someone return your call, or you may contact our communications staff directly at [phone number]."

If you have any questions on our communications policy, feel free to contact [CCT Leader, contact information].

While existing and new employees should be initially briefed and trained on the organization's media policy, the policy must be re-issued:

◆ In a crisis situation
◆ During heightened alert
◆ At the beginning of a particular weather cycle, such as hurricane, winter storm or monsoon seasons
◆ When staff are promoted

During an incident, distribute a summary document of the policies and procedures to ensure that more employees read the document and understand why they are being told to review the policies.

3.4.1 Approval process to release information
An established process for timely review and approval of all external materials and statements is critical to a successful communications response. The media may call before the organization even knows about the crisis, or may arrive at the incident scene before a communications staff member. Therefore, maintain a robust review and approval process to ensure that the organization can provide information to the media as quickly as possible. The communications plan must assign a specific amount of authority to the spokesperson that will first speak to the media. **If that person is able to release confirmed basic data, the media will be less likely to try to find alternative sources of information.**

The CDC, US Coast Guard and US Air Force have public information clearance procedures to consider including:

◆ If the organization has not yet developed an answer to an apparently urgent question, explain to the media and public that information is forthcoming

◆ Have **three members** of the CCT review every document before its release:
- A person responsible for the organization's reputation, typically the CCT Leader
- A person directly responsible for the information being cleared
- A person with subject-matter expertise on any technical information within the document

◆ **Designate backup personnel for each function**

◆ **Clear documents in person, simultaneously and in private** with the designated review team. If that is not possible, the CCT Leader must coordinate with those team members to ensure document clearance is as rapid and private as possible.

◆ **As a part of the clearance 'test':**
- Focus on any areas still in question and avoid speculation
- Verify that the compiled information answers media/public/stakeholder questions and also covers points on which questions are anticipated
- Integrate key messages into the document for release (See *Chapter 6: Messages and Strategy* for guidance on creating key messages)

- Ensure that each review member is comfortable with the possibility that any part of the text could appear as a headline in the media
- ◆ **Establish a timetable for clearance** of information, distinguishing between 'must-know' and less urgent 'nice-to-know' information. Remember, it is better to release partial information with the caveat that more is forthcoming than to release none at all.
- ◆ **Create pre-cleared key messages** during the planning process to expedite the clearing process. If the organization knows that it may have to deal with losses of life or property, carefully craft possible response language beforehand. **Tailor these to the specific circumstances of an incident** before release.
- ◆ Determine what is **non-releasable,** to ensure the protection of the following information and **liability of the organization**:

General
- Classified material
- Details of law enforcement response
- Matters under investigation, apart from judicial proceedings
- Specific information covered by statute (such as certain financial records)
- Personal data of victims, family members, employees, service officials including: names, age, residence, health history/status

- Identity of victims before family members have been informed
- Identity of children involved

Operations

- Internal discussion documents: memoranda, e-mails, meeting summaries
- Response measures: evacuation procedures, threat response policy
- Human resources: employee training, background checks
- Information technology: disaster recovery plan, mitigation and recovery procedures
- Vulnerability assessments: checklists of areas assessed, identified deficiencies, mitigation of those deficiencies
- Company/sector statistics: numbers of people, goods, data and/or services managed, processed, produced, tracked and so on

For further guidance on creating crisis response policies on protecting facilities, personnel and information security, see *Jane's Workplace Security Handbook*.

Financial

- **Proprietary or confidential** business information
- **Financial projections:** these may create unrealistic earnings expectations. Instead, present general information about the

organization's state of operations: customers, performance, past relevant experiences.

- **Unconfirmed product availability:** financial analysts make predictions partly based on new product lines and there is a risk to breaking a delivery promise
- **Large-scale customer relationships:** negative press on a corporate relationship can increase tensions and/or depress the stock value of one or both companies
- **Potential partnerships:** comments may affect the other parties, especially during discussions on mergers or acquisitions
- **Status of research and development capabilities:** revealing internal strategies will raise performance expectations and give ideas to competitors

Source: The Making of a Corporate Spokesperson – Media Interview Technique, The Loeb Group, 1999

In general, do not release this information, since liability suits may result – especially if the organization cannot confirm a claimed standard of care for operations. Only use this information with the media and key stakeholders when it is clearly appropriate. For example, if a company's operations statistics show its safety record to be high compared to the industry average, then this information may be helpful in establishing credibility.

Joint operations

- If the organization partners with other entities on an ongoing basis or as a part of its crisis response, **designate a chain of command for the release of information**
- Designate **different levels and types** of response as well as release schedules for each
- Document, distribute and **update the procedures** as agreed
- **Conduct exercises to test cooperative structure** and ensure seamless cooperation in the event of an incident

See section *3.7.1 Creating relationships with potential communications partners* for more information on coordinating joint operations.

Overall, pre-clearing what is releasable information will facilitate efficient crisis communications, especially during the **initial phase of an incident.** For quick reference, see section *10.1.4 Information release clearance and parameters.*

3.5 Media policy for employees

3.5.1 Staff training

The CCT Leader and members should attend media training seminars to hone writing and speaking skills throughout the year. Budget permitting, CCT members and potential operational spokespeople should practice delivering statements and answering questions on camera and review their performance. Doing so will allow spokespeople to know and improve on how they appear to the public.

Keep in mind that the CCT Leader or members will not always be the only people in an organization speaking to the media. When an organization announces a major new policy, for example, the head of the organization, not a CCT member, should be the speaker.

When information to be passed on to the media includes technical details about an organization's operations, staff with operational expertise may need to assist the CCT Leader in communicating this information. In some cases, operational staff may have to communicate with the media directly. Communicating technical information in a widely understandable format during a crisis can be challenging. The media's time and space constraints severely limit the level of specificity, even when details are essential to the organization's communications response. Understanding and adapting to media constraints beforehand can make the difference between a successful communications response and a failed one. See *Chapter 2: Pre-incident Media Relations* for a detailed look at how the media respond to a crisis and what constraints they face.

Quick training

A US Coast Guard patrol boat seized three vessels carrying a total of one ton of cocaine. As the crew brought the seized vessels, drugs and smugglers into their Miami Beach, Florida headquarters, they were told that the *CBS Morning Show* had previously arranged to broadcast live from the base on US counter-narcotics efforts. The commander of the boat, Commander James McPherson, was to be interviewed but he did not have previous experience in media relations. A Coast Guard PAO quickly trained him, providing a media brief, talking points and key messages. Immediately after tying up the patrol boat, CDR McPherson walked off the pier and gave media interviews. CDR McPherson was able to give a successful interview and the event received very positive press. He was subsequently given more extensive media training.

Source: CDR James McPherson, Chief, Media Relations, USCG

There will also be times when people who experienced a crisis first-hand should speak to the press. Someone who saved a life, found a lost child or led a successful mission will often tell the story the best. The media want to hear from these people, because they add human interest to the coverage. **It is therefore imperative to train all staff in media relations. This includes conducting practice interviews and press conferences.**

Media gather at the pier at the US Naval Base in Guantanamo Bay, Cuba to document interdicted Haitian migrants being repatriated Source: US Coast Guard photo by Robin Ressler. ***2002***/0535636

3.5.2 Crisis communications training exercises
Include crisis communications functions in crisis response exercises, rather than practicing them separately. This way, crisis response and crisis communication functions will be integrated just as they would be in an actual incident. Role-play with media operations and expectations to prepare staff for situations they may confront in an actual crisis. For realism, develop a crisis scenario that the organization could actually encounter. Take members of the CCT, senior leaders and other selected staff through each phase of a crisis situation: initial, continuing, diminishing, resolution, evaluation and recognition.

Incident-based training

The US Air Force public affairs office at Langley Air Force Base trains senior staff on crisis communications response to an aircraft accident. The participants have included: base fire chief and fire officials, safety experts, engineers (who help with crash clean-up and rebuilding efforts), medical experts, base security experts, chaplains and on-scene commanders. Based on that planning, the public affairs office was able to send out a press release within an hour of an F-15 Fighter crash.

Langley F-15 crashes off Virginia coast

LANGLEY AIR FORCE BASE, Va. — An F-15C from the 1st Fighter Wing at Langley crashed at approximately 9:45 am today 60 to 70 miles off the Virginia Beach, Va, shore.

The pilot, 1st Lt David Nyikos, assigned to the 94th Fighter Squadron, ejected and was picked up by a US Coast Guard search and rescue helicopter. He was brought to Langley's hospital and was listed in good condition after spending less than an hour in a rubber raft.

Nyikos was piloting one of two 1st FW aircraft conducting routine training at the time of the incident.

A board of officers will investigate the accident.

Since the staff was trained in media relations, the Air Force had information ready to explain the investigation process, how an ejection seat works and the great lengths the military goes through to ensure safety.

Source: Captain Joseph Della Vedova, US Air Force Public Affairs

3.6 Communications resources

Crisis Communication Teams typically operate with few resources and employees before a crisis occurs. Instituting planning procedures and demonstrating the importance of crisis communications as a part of crisis response through material preparation, exercises and training sessions can help justify investments in communications capabilities. **The CCT must emphasize to senior management that an organization will end up paying more for a poorly executed communications response then for the initial investments to equip a communications staff.**

3.6.1 Crisis Center

Establish a staff member to equip and maintain a Crisis Center where the CCT can handle internal and external communications needs. Situating the Crisis Center close to other key areas, such as the Command Post and the press conference area, will ensure that information flows as quickly and smoothly as possible. An alternate site should also be identified if the designated room becomes temporarily unavailable.

Equip the Crisis Center with the following:

◆ Telephones, with designated incoming and outgoing lines
◆ Contact lists for organization, authorities, media and other stakeholder groups
◆ Computers connected to the organization's network

- Web access and e-mail
- Printers
- Fax machines
- Back-up generators, batteries, food, water and medical kits
- Speakerphone for conference calls, with multilateral hook-up capabilities to connect many parties at once
- Large whiteboard(s) to display updated information and a chronology of the situation, so that the entire crisis response team stays abreast of developments. (This is particularly helpful when intense media interest necessitates having several spokespersons.)
- Televisions
- Cable hook-up and backup such as satellite or UHF/VHF antennas to monitor media coverage
- Video cassette recorders to tape broadcasts
- Two-way radios and scanners on emergency response tactical radio frequencies, to monitor operations
- Office supplies: pens, paper, computer disks, phone cords, a mirror for spokespersons to review their appearance and so on
- Internal policy documents

3.6.2 Contracting communications staff

Establish a protocol with the finance office or partner organizations to bring in temporary staff to assist the

CCT if needed, especially for 24-hour operations. Additional staff may include:

◆ Translators
◆ Website development support staff
◆ Subject-matter experts, representatives from respective trade associations
◆ Public relations consultants
◆ Videographers/photographers
◆ Other office support staff as appropriate

Multilingual skills

It is an organization's interest to be aware of any special language needs among their stakeholders and the general public, in the local community or abroad. In larger metropolitan areas and/or where the major news networks have operations, international media organizations with affiliate stations or local bureaus broadcast in their respective languages back to a specific country or region.

In South Florida, for example, 57 percent of the population is Spanish-speaking. Therefore, the news program of a Spanish-language local news program has garnered higher ratings than all English newscasts combined.

Meeting multilingual needs

The 1997 'Super Bowl Sunday' flood in San Jose, California required the evacuation and sheltering of residents across five neighborhoods simultaneously. The residents spoke at least three different primary languages other then English. Bilingual staff members from various City departments accompanied public safety personnel into the flooded areas to explain flood safety precautions and evacuation plans using loud speakers mounted on police vehicles. The Emergency Public Information Officers addressed the non-English language media by using bilingual City staff as interpreters and spokespersons.

The Office of Emergency Services (OES) obtained public health precautions from the County Public Health Officer then translated them into multiple languages. The Disaster Application Center was staffed with bilingual City employees offering assistance for four language/cultural groups (English, Spanish, Vietnamese and Cambodian) to assist potential applicants in language- and culture-friendly ways.

Source: Dr. Frances Edwards-Winslow, Director of Emergency Preparedness, City of San Jose, California

3.7 Cooperation with other organizations

Before a crisis occurs, an organization should foster good relations with the media, emergency responders, the local community, stakeholders and elected/public officials.

Establishing those relationships before a crisis is critical to ensuring an integrated response, since almost all crises involve multiple organizations and response agencies. Coordinating communications across organizations is vital for ensuring that media and stakeholders receive information quickly and accurately.

3.7.1 Creating relationships with potential communications partners

During a crisis involving several response agencies, a Joint Information Center (JIC) may be necessary to manage information dissemination and relationships. To ensure the JIC functions smoothly, the CCT Leader should reach out to other organizations in both the public and the private sector that are willing to participate in joint crisis communications.

◆ Create a call list of other CCT Leaders in related organizations, industries or the organization's geographic area
◆ Organize a meeting for area CCT Leaders to discuss common threats, goals, strategies, experiences and so on
◆ Establish a CCT group composed of members from each organization or join an existing one. (A large

number of state/province and nationwide CCT
Leader groups exist.)
◆ Invite other CCT Leaders to tour the organization's
facilities
◆ Create a system to track finances in the event a JIC
is activated and resources are shared or require
reimbursement

Proactive joint communications
Ronald Reagan Washington National Airport in
Washington, DC experienced a problem with the water
supplied to the airport. Routine tests showed the
presence of e.coli bacteria.

While subsequent tests proved negative, the
Metropolitan Washington Airports Authority (MWAA)
knew it had to issue a press release to inform the public
coming to the airport, per a federal environmental law
requiring public notice at water fountains and in
lavatories whenever a sample tested positive for e.coli.

MWAA worked with the state environmental and the
water authority staffs in developing the press release
and coordinating spokespersons for the various aspects
of the situation. This cooperation allowed MWAA to
present the facts about the airport's water safety and
avoid any public confusion.

Source: Tara Hamilton, Public Affairs Manager, MWAA

Upon forming relationships with other CCT's and/or Team Leaders, run joint exercises and drills to determine JIC procedures and jurisdictional boundaries. Even if a crisis is not occurring, organizations can cooperate to inform the public **proactively** on an issue. This may be as minor as contacting other organizations to confirm technical information or collaborating on a document for release.

In some cases, organizations may not have the time or opportunity to meet CCT Leaders and/or spokespersons from other organizations before a crisis occurs. In the event of a crisis, contact the other organizations as soon as possible and suggest convening a meeting with their CCT or Team Leaders in order to begin planning for information dissemination.

It is important to understand that in any JIC operation, the interests of the various parties may differ, especially when public and private organizations are involved. Different organizations may want to communicate with the media in different ways and with different messages.

For more caveats and procedures on setting up a JIC, during an incident see section *6.3 Creating a Joint Information Center (JIC)*.

The following case study illustrates the need to incorporate the planning procedures described in this chapter. **Any incident, small or large, can attract a**

large media presence and create a public desire for accurate, reassuring information.

Quick response to an anthrax scare

On August 21, 2002, several people were reported to be coughing, sneezing and having difficulty breathing at a security checkpoint at Miami International Airport. The office for Miami-Dade County Fire Rescue Public Affairs (MDFR PA) implemented its action plan.

Learning of the response dispatch from a Public Information Officer (PIO), the Bureau Chief sent the PIO to the airport who alerted the airport Public Affairs (PA) office while traveling. The MDFR PA office started to receive local media inquiries within five minutes of the response dispatch to the site.

The PA office was soon inundated with national and international news requests for live phone interviews. Two staff members managed the media calls, sorting the requests by type (English, Spanish, local, state, national, international) for PA office spokespersons on call. The Bureau Chief conducted the first interview and established the key messages for the other spokespersons to use, in both English and Spanish.

Even though the PIO arrived on scene to obtain information from the incident commander in 11 minutes, rumors were rampant and broadcast journalists were on-air live outside the terminal. The incident was

---

probably due to a discarded pepper spray can going off in the trash and not the original speculation of anthrax that had fueled the intense press response.

This incident, while newsworthy, would probably not have received such attention had anthrax attacks not occurred in the US during 2001. Existing policy development and preparation allowed the MDFR PA team to quell fears quickly. Its effective response involved these key elements:

◆ Access to and frequent monitoring of emergency service dispatches
◆ Quick decision to send a PIO to the scene
◆ Notification/cooperation with airport PA
  • Established clear jurisdictional boundaries with MDFR speaking solely on fire/rescue and hazardous materials operations, and airport officials speaking only on airport operations
  • Coordinated simultaneous sound bites on scene
◆ Pre-incident procedures prepared a quick response to 40 live phone interviews for the local, national and international media within a two-hour period

The well-executed response prevented delayed flights and panic among passengers, family members, business colleagues and related effects such as missed appointments and increased airport/airline operational costs.

Overall, the successful implementation of this communications response plan displays the need to prepare, test, execute and evaluate a crisis communications response strategy **in the high-risk security environment reported throughout the around-the-clock media cycle.** As noted, confusion, speculation, quick media response time surfaced as elements of the incident.

For specific steps on implementing the crisis communications response plan, see *Chapter 4: Response Procedures Checklist, Chapter 5: Gathering and Verifying Information, Chapter 6: Messages and Strategy, Chapter 7: Engaging Key Stakeholders* and *Chapter 8: Working with the Media.*

CHAPTER 4: RESPONSE PROCEDURES CHECKLISTS

CHAPTER 4: RESPONSE PROCEDURES CHECKLIST

4.1 Introduction

Through the initial, continuing, diminishing and resolution phases of the crisis, **many procedures need to be implemented simultaneously to maximize efficiency and respond to multiple demands.** This chapter provides a **checklist** that details all of the steps a Crisis Communications Team (CCT) will need to consider when developing an **effective crisis communications response.** This comprehensive checklist will reference appropriate sections of the other response chapters that provide greater depth on each area.

4.1.1 Seven-step communications response plan

Throughout the crisis, the CCT needs to formulate a consistent message and disseminate it both internally and externally. To achieve these goals, the CCT must carry out its response plan in tandem with the overall crisis response and recovery. The CCT Leader should manage implementing the communications component of the crisis response plan using seven steps:

(1) Activate the CCT
(2) Gather and verify information
(3) Assess the gravity of the crisis
(4) Identify key stakeholders
(5) Implement a communications strategy

(6) Develop external materials
(7) Inform partners, stakeholders and media

4.2 Initial phase
The CCT Leader will oversee the immediate response procedures and will delegate responsibilities to available staff.

4.2.1 Internal response: immediate

☐ Notify senior leadership of available facts

☐ Dispatch a CCT member to the scene of the crisis **to gather additional information, not to speak**

☐ Notify the CCT and direct it to assemble in **Crisis Center**

☐ Dispatch any additional communications staff as necessary: videographer/photographer, translator

4.2.2 External relations response: immediate

☐ **Prepare facts** for initial interviews/press release

☐ **Obtain clearance** to issue press release

☐ **Fax and email initial press release** with available facts to the following groups and state that more information will be released as available:
  • Partner organizations
  • Emergency services' communications officers
  • Wire services

☐ **Identify spokesperson(s) for initial** interview(s): CCT Leader/members

---

☐ **Identify backup spokesperson(s)**

☐ **Respond to initial queries** to confirm basic information and include key messages if possible

See section *6.4 Key messages*, section *8.4 Press releases*, section *8.6 Interview guidelines* and section *10.1.4 Information release clearance and parameters* checklist

4.2.3 Assign crisis communications responsibilities

☐ Information-gathering liaisons:
  - Response team/operations center
  - Stakeholders
  - Partner organizations
  - Internal operational or outside consultants/ subject matter experts

☐ Researcher

☐ Media query calls/media log maintenance

☐ Media monitoring

☐ Writing/editing news releases, talking points, fact sheets

☐ Website updates

☐ Crisis Center office/logistics/support

☐ Establish estimated time for next CCT meeting

See section *5.3 Confirm information*, section *6.5 Incident-based situation assessment and considerations* for research guidance, section *8.5.3 Indoor press conference area and Crisis Center* for office supply and technology needs and section *10.2.1 Media Log* for a template

4.2.4 Determine level of response/external cooperation

☐ Discuss verified information

☐ **Assess the gravity** of the situation

☐ Identify involved parties/stakeholders and **prioritize attention to possible victims and families**

See *Chapter 7: Engaging Key Stakeholders* for guidance on different groups

4.3 Continuing phase

The continuing phase represents the second-stage crisis response and confirms the level of attention and resources needed. This attention may or may not be for a sustained amount of time. The CCT will need to determine **the type of approach and level of activation.** The following procedures represent a comprehensive approach and full activation.

4.3.1 Communications approach

☐ **Establish a Joint Information Center (JIC)**
   • Advise the media on location of the JIC

☐ Review initial **approach guidelines**

☐ **Create key messages** for stakeholders and for the public via the media

☐ Consider **incident-specific responses**:
- Natural disaster
- Human-caused hazard
- Mechanical/technological malfunction

See section *6.2 Approach parameters* for guidelines on message development, section *6.3 Creating a Joint Information Center (JIC)* and section *6.4 Key messages* to create sound bites

4.3.2 Level of activation

☐ **Plan a press conference** to disseminate a significant announcement quickly

☐ **Issue media advisory**

☐ **Press conference preparation**
- Within the CCT, identify and prepare speakers for questions based on situation assessment
- Create visuals, press kits
- Identify language requirements and assign staff accordingly

☐ **Outdoor press conference area/ communications vehicle**
- **Equip press conference area and communications vehicle** as soon as possible
- If possible, have the CCT **inform media of location** while the CCT Leader or main spokesperson is en route to scene
- **If confronted by media upon arrival:**
  - State name and title

- Give a brief synopsis of the event: who, what, where, when, why
- Use key messages
- **Identify media staging** area in front of outdoor press office
- **Explain media access**/ground rules
- **Announce the briefing** schedule and if the spokesperson(s) will be receiving questions

☐ **Indoor press conference area**
- **Situate press conference area away from CCT Crisis Center to ensure privacy**
- Place a CCT member in the press office with media **at all times,** if possible
- Equip room if not already prepared

☐ **Press conference procedures**
- Have the CCT Leader manage the event
- **Establish event schedule and ground rules at beginning of press conference**
- **Conclude speaker statements with assurances** and answer questions, if scheduled to do so
- Depending on the incident and its progression, **announce time of next press conference.** Otherwise, state that additional information will be released as developments are confirmed.
- **Direct press to organization and/or crisis response website** for updates and additional background material
- Announce CCT office **phone number for press use only**

☐ **Schedule interviews**
- Fulfill interview requests as soon as possible depending on media concentration: **same day, next morning and/or between or after press conference(s)**
- If conducting one-on-one interviews between press conferences, be consistent and fair. **Do not offer exclusives.**
- **Obtain interview details from media log**
- Keep in mind **message, approach and demeanor guidelines**

See section *8.5.1 Preparation* for press conferences, section *8.5.3 Indoor press conference area and Crisis Center,* section *8.5.4 Outdoor press conference area* to create an outdoor press office and equip a CCT vehicle, section *8.5.6 Procedures during a press conference,* section *8.6 Interview guidelines* and section *10.2.3 Media advisory* template

4.4 Diminishing phase

After the immediacy of the crisis passes, the frequency of press conferences will decrease according to the progress made towards achieving a resolution. The CCT should regularly reassess if the initial strategy remains sound within the **seven-step response** presented at the start of this chapter.

Depending on the analysis, **adjust communications** to key stakeholders and **make or request corrections** as necessary.

See section *8.3.1 Making corrections* for guidance on pursuing corrections with the media.

4.5 Resolution

A crisis does not always end on day one. Often, a crisis — and its implications — can extend over weeks, months or even years. **Last remaining** updates serve to call an end to the crisis if a concrete resolution is possible.

Either hold a final press conference if the end to an incident is significant or issue a press release to confirm final details on the incident.

4.5.1 Final press conference

☐ Declare end of crisis

☐ Provide final details of incident

☐ Disseminate information on those involved

☐ Repeat key messages:
- Empathy for losses
- Recognition of rescue/response effort
- Recovery plan
- Future steps to avoid/prepare for incident repeat

See *Chapter 9: Post-incident Management*

CHAPTER 5: GATHERING AND VERIFYING INFORMATION

CHAPTER 5: GATHERING AND VERIFYING INFORMATION

5.1 Introduction

When an incident occurs, an organization must immediately play the internal role of a 'reporter' in compiling, confirming and assessing information as it becomes available. **Effective communications during the first 24 hours of a crisis will establish the organization's credibility to manage the entire response and recovery operation.** This is especially true for the media, since reporters create their 'leads' en route to the incident or soon after arriving. John Curran, Home Assignment Editor for the BBC Newsgathering department of the asserts:

> "Too often chief executives turn up days later or not at all. They hide...then they give furtive, fruitless news conferences miles from the scene. We reckon on handling one major breaker a month on domestic or foreign news. When you get one you can usually tell within 24 hours whether the boss of a big organization that's in the news is leading it or just managing it."

This chapter will discuss procedures to gather and confirm information as soon as possible. Keep in mind that these steps may occur simultaneously:

◆ Activate the Crisis Communications Team (CCT)

◆ Confirm information
◆ Assess the gravity of the crisis
◆ Identify key stakeholders

5.2 Activate the Crisis Communications Team

The CCT Leader must determine if the group should meet immediately to assess the incident or if individual members should first work on their own to collect information. From then on, the team must periodically reassess whether it should work as a group or should delegate tasks to individuals. Ideally, team members should have radios/walkie-talkies because land-line telephones and cell phones may be out of operation.

The following is an example of possible team members needed to assist in the communications response:

◆ Communications
◆ Operations
◆ Government relations
◆ Community relations
◆ Legal
◆ Investor relations
◆ Relevant outside consultants (communications, legal, security)
◆ Senior leadership, if the severity of the situation requires their attention
◆ Support staff:
    • Media queries/media log maintenance
    • Media monitoring

- Research
- Editing/writing
- Website updates
- Crisis Center and press conference area

5.3 Confirm information
Assign duties to CCT members and **support staff** to verify information as it becomes available:

◆ Information-gathering liaisons for the following areas:
  - Crisis response team/operations center
  - Stakeholder groups
  - Partner organizations
  - Outside consultants, subject matter experts, membership associations
◆ Research
◆ Media monitoring

5.3.1 Sorting the information
The following are basic assessment questions to help determine the severity of a crisis:

Initial information
◆ What specific events occurred or are expected?
◆ Where did or will they occur?
◆ When did or will they occur?
◆ Why did or will they happen?

◆ Who is or will be affected? (Are children involved?)
◆ What action should the public take?

Response activities
◆ What has already been done to control the situation?
◆ Is there remaining danger?
◆ Has the affected area been secured?
◆ Have proper authorities been notified, such as emergency crews, police, fire and/or other law enforcement/regulatory authorities?
◆ What actions have the authorities taken?
◆ How can public and employees obtain information – through a hotline, website, scheduled meetings?

Public health concerns
◆ Was anyone injured or killed, or what is the potential for injury or death?
◆ If there is a fatality, how and when was someone killed?
◆ Do the victims' families know what happened? Is the organization responsible for informing relatives?
◆ Was the victim an employee or member of the community?
◆ Are any individuals still at risk?
◆ What are the names, ages, addresses, family information and hospital location for the people affected?
◆ If a victim is an employee, what is his/her title, job

description and length of service with the
organization?
◆ Was there a rescue, who conducted it?

Facility impact
◆ Was an organization's facility involved? If so, what
kind of facility? What was its function?
◆ Was the facility damaged?
◆ Were operations interrupted?
◆ Who will be affected by the incident?
◆ How much will this event cost to mitigate?

Media interest
◆ Have rumor control numbers been established?
◆ Are the media aware of the incident; are they on
site?
◆ Is the media coverage being monitored and taped
for accuracy review?
◆ Have the press called and are queries being
logged?
◆ Has a website been set up to post background
information?

See *Chapter 6: Messages and Strategy* for incident-
based research questions specific to natural disasters,
human-caused hazards or mechanical malfunctions.

5.4 Assess the gravity of the crisis
Once the CCT collects and verifies the information and
has reviewed special considerations, determine the

gravity of the emergency. This is done in consultation with the CCT information-gathering liaisons. For example, the crisis response team liaison would need to obtain the **situation reports (SITREPs)** or updated chronologies of crisis and response events issued at regular intervals from the command post. The other CCT liaisons (stakeholder groups, partner organizations, outside consultants/subject matter experts/trade associations) should provide as full an account as possible of the incident and its implications.

Distribute the situation assessment in a consistent format to all members of the CCT so that the entire group is working from the same set of facts. When it is appropriate, the CCT Leader and crisis response leader (or incident commander) should also convey the information to other staff, such as the senior leadership. **In all situations, it is extremely important to verify and double-check all facts, particularly in highly sensitive cases.**

5.5 Identify key stakeholders
Depending on the nature of the incident, it may be necessary to **identify affected groups in order to form appropriately targeted key messages**. Be attentive to differences among the messages to various stakeholder groups.

If the incident involves sensitive information vital to the well-being and safety of **specific groups – especially**

if they are victims, children and families – make every effort to develop materials for them before informing the media. People should never learn of their loved ones' injury or death through the media. Meet stakeholders in person with verified information, the organization's response to address their needs and/or recourse options available to them. See *Chapter 6: Messages and Strategy* and *Chapter 7: Engaging Key Stakeholders* for procedures on creating materials and services for groups the crisis affects.

CHAPTER 6: MESSAGES AND STRATEGY

CHAPTER 6: MESSAGES AND STRATEGY

6.1 Introduction

Once the Crisis Communications Team (CCT) has gathered and verified the incident information and has prioritized stakeholders, the team must decide on a level of response and on means of communication. While careful consideration of the strategy and messages is important, time is also of the essence. **How an organization handles the first 24 hours of a crisis situation will establish its reputation for the entire response and recovery operation.** Therefore, assume a 'worst-case scenario' when developing the response strategy. While every situation is unique, it is imperative to **balance carefully the demands of internal management and external communications**.

This chapter will discuss procedures and the nuances of the following:

◆ Approach parameters
◆ Creating a Joint Information Center (JIC)
◆ Forming key messages
◆ Conducting an incident-based situation assessment for natural disasters, human-caused hazards and/or mechanical malfunctions

6.2 Approach parameters

If the situation does not require the authorities to respond, an organization may implement **proactive communication** to all stakeholders in some circumstances. In other situations, it may make more sense to take a more **reactive approach** as questions arise. Factors to consider in taking a proactive approach include potential legal liabilities/issues as well as the nature and gravity of the incident. Whether an organization takes a reactive or proactive approach, keep these guidelines in mind while crafting the materials and talking points:

◆ **Display concern and dedication to resolve the crisis:** never minimize the severity of the crisis and offer public reassurance when appropriate

◆ **Notify families first:** do not discuss any injuries or deaths until families of the victims have been notified

◆ **Establish order and credibility:** the public will tolerate emergencies but **not** inaccurate information, mixed messages, unwarranted silence or evasiveness

◆ **Be the first source of information:** release verified information immediately. Otherwise, the media, working on deadlines, will find another source.

◆ **Admit 'I don't know':** when the information is not confirmed. Do not hesitate to say that an answer is not yet available. Give assurance that an answer will be forthcoming.

◆ **Maintain equal media access:** do not release relevant information to media organizations selectively

◆ **Issue key messages:** in 10- to 12-word sound bite increments. Convey the organization's concern and view on the nature of the incident and response. Use discretion when creating messages for stakeholders, and if necessary, tell them to take specific actions.

◆ **Communicate technical details clearly:** educating people during a crisis is difficult. Use visual aids, such as charts, graphs and timelines. Avoid jargon and define any unavoidable technical terms.

◆ **Stay positive, but realistic:** recovery begins with the confidence the team displays during the crisis

◆ **Never speculate**

◆ **Do not discuss undetermined issues:** focus on the evolving issues at hand. Damages, causes, blame and so on are addressed after investigations are complete

◆ **Do not provide proprietary or sensitive information**

See section *8.6 Interview guidelines* for specific procedures on interacting with the press.

6.3 Creating a Joint Information Center (JIC)

If the situation requires more than one organization to respond, or if the organization needs resource assistance, consider establishing a JIC to create a cohesive communications response. **It is essential that the lead agency determine who will be the spokesperson for the JIC.** The on-scene response coordinator (or incident commander) will usually determine who manages the JIC. As soon as possible, implement these procedures:

◆ **Obtain consensus** from the CCT – and senior leadership, if necessary – **that a JIC is needed**
◆ Contact CCT Leaders at the relevant organizations with the verified incident details and **invite them to join the JIC**
◆ **Establish a central Crisis Center** near the incident site from which to conduct operations and field press inquiries:
  • Establish equipment and standard operating procedures
◆ **Establish clear areas of responsibility:**
  • Lead organization
  • Specific subject areas each organization will cover. **Do not answer questions on behalf of another organization.**
  • Primary spokesperson(s) from each subject area

◆ **Create a process to distribute internal communications:**

- Standardize situation report (SITREP) briefing times
- Distribute media schedules: press releases, press conferences, interviews
- Brief senior staff: give them updates before press conferences and interagency meetings
- Analyze bias, spin and any press errors from media monitoring
- Ensure smooth shift changes: make sure the new shift has updated information and reads the previous releases to maintain sequential flow of information
- Prepare for expected VIP visits

◆ Implement a system to **track finances** if reimbursement is anticipated

If the JIC involves both private and public organizations, usually the government agency leads the response and recovery operations. Once the crisis subsides and the public agency completes its operations, the private organization takes over for the post-incident management. Throughout, organizations must avoid using this authoritative venue to promote its and/or the industry's own interests.

Aircraft crash response

When a civilian aircraft crashed at Langley US Air Force Base, killing two pilots, the Air Force and the National Transportation Safety Board (NTSB) needed to cooperate on the response since civilians were involved.

The two organizations convened a meeting and clearly defined their respective roles and responsibilities about the communications response.

The organizations worked together to inform the public about the accident. When communicating to the media, the NTSB discussed the accident investigation and the Air Force discussed the impact on the base and efforts it took to assist in the investigation.

Source: Captain Joseph Della Vedova, US Air Force Public Affairs

6.4 Key messages

An organization must first develop a set of key messages – no more than three or four points. Two types of key messages will be discussed. **Position key messages** convey the organization's view on the nature of the incident and the response. **Instructional key messages** direct the stakeholders to take specific action. It is critical that the CCT communicate a consistent message platform to all stakeholders. Therefore, the same key messages should be woven throughout all external and internal communications materials.

6.4.1 Position key messages

These short messages must be part of all communications, to ensure that the organization's empathy and credibility are heard. For example, Rudi Giuliani, former Mayor of New York City, received high praise for his ability to reassure the public that local, state and federal government agencies were doing everything possible to facilitate the recovery from the attacks on the World Trade Center. Key messages describe the organization's position – not just raw data. As press releases, interviews and/or press conferences will expound on the causes, effects and future options; **use position messages to calm the public.** The messages should have these qualities:

◆ Possesses positive or neutral outlook
◆ Uses less than 12-word increments
◆ Spoken in 10-12 second increments
◆ Highlights mission of the organization and its dedication to resolving the crisis, using theme words:
  • Condolences
  • Care, concern, reassurance
  • Response time
  • Training
  • Cooperation
  • Preparedness/expertise

- Security
- Customer-oriented
- Quality work/safety record
- Heroism
- Dedication
- Enforcement/compliance with laws

Public organizations may use additional position messages based on the function of their agencies. Positions may also be developed using the organization's mission statement. Well-known **private entities may consider using adjectives associated with their brand name** to reinforce their capability in mitigating further damage and their dedication to customer service and safety.

Although key message space and time constraints may appear daunting, recall how short quotes are in print and broadcast media reports. **Sound bites will generate a more cohesive message than a long response that the press will most likely edit.** Press conferences and live interviews will allow for more expansive communication.

When answering questions, 'bridge' or connect the response to a position key message. Bridging can also involve transition phrases, such as:

◆   More importantly...
◆   The real issue is...

◆ The fact of the matter is...
◆ What is interesting...

The following example from the US Coast Guard shows how raw data must be crafted into clear statements that confirm vital information while communicating a key message and the organization's overall mission.

Incident raw data: capsized 22-foot pleasure boat; six-foot seas; four miles east of Cape May; on-scene in less than 15 minutes; man and his two sons wearing lifejackets; survivors filed float (boating) plan with wife/mother.

Public statement: 'The US Coast Guard rescued three survivors today after their boat sank four miles east of Cape May *(factual answer)*. This rescue illustrates to boaters the importance of filing a float plan, having the right safety gear and wearing life jackets *(position message)*. The Coast Guard saves 4,000 lives in search and rescue missions per year *(mission)*.'

Source: CDR Steve Sapp, 'US Coast Guard Officer-in-Charge Course,' US Coast Guard

6.4.2 Instructional key messages
These messages are designed to direct the public's response to immediate public safety concerns:

◆ Evacuations: weather, fires, chemical spills

◆ Infectious disease, medical advisories
◆ Terrorist activity/alerts
◆ Recall for a dangerous product
◆ Other large-scale emergencies

Instructional key messages also include public safety announcements about such things as weather and traffic conditions during holidays or mass gatherings for sporting events or cultural activities. Mass gatherings often have higher incidents of accidents related to congested traffic, heat exhaustion, dehydration, alcohol poisoning, gate-crashing and physical altercations.

Other messages may alert citizens to watch for escaped criminals or assailants, and may list hotline numbers to report any sightings or other related events.

6.5 Incident-based situation assessment and considerations

Responders often need to address specific investigative questions and follow specific response procedures, depending on the incident. Some situations require the CCT to be aware of special considerations with stakeholders, the media and/or the crisis response team.

The following material covers communications plans for natural disasters, human-caused hazards and mechanical/technological malfunctions.

NOTE: In the next sections, solely the Crisis Communications Team's functions and responsibilities are discussed. In no way should the following interfere with tactical operations designed to eliminate or minimize the threat.

6.6 Natural disasters

Natural disasters affect many sectors of the community. Work with affected groups on pertinent developments and the safety instructions. These groups may include:

◆ Emergency services
◆ Weather services
◆ Elected local, county, provincial/state and federal officials
◆ Utilities: electric, water, gas
◆ Telecommunications
◆ Transportation
◆ Businesses
◆ Schools
◆ Media

During natural disasters, the public looks to the government and private emergency-response agencies for leadership. Businesses will also need to provide information regarding the early-leave policy and impact on operations.

Sudden events, such as tornadoes, earthquakes, flash

floods and outbreaks of infectious diseases, **require a quick response** from the CCT.

Unfolding events, such as hurricanes or typhoons, allow much more time to prepare. For these, use a different set of procedures.

During both sudden and unfolding natural disasters, organizations must offer information to the media and/or community **proactively:**

◆ **Currently available information:** regular, pertinent environmental conditions and warnings disseminated via radio, television, and online and hardcopy print media as well as organization website

◆ **Preparatory tasks for the public:** stocking food, water, flashlights, batteries, radios, medical supplies

◆ **Response updates:** assurances to the public of preventive/response steps that the organization – typically emergency services – is being executed

◆ **Additional information:** announce rumor control measures, such as hotline number and incident-specific website

◆ **Message cohesion:** tone of announcements must be in concert with local weather service and other response authorities

◆ **Leave policy:** create a notification policy to employees, and parents with children in schools, directing them to go to their homes to avoid bad weather conditions

While incidents such as hurricanes and typhoons differ from tornadoes and earthquakes in how fast they occur, both will become **medium- to long-term operations.** The CCT must continue to follow the previous steps. Generally, the public will want to hear in-depth advice and information throughout the entire incident cycle.

Prepare a rapid assessment of critical facts:

◆ Is there a continued threat?
◆ Where is the damage?
◆ Who is affected; what are the language needs?
◆ What are the authorities doing?
◆ What should the public be doing?
◆ What should employees be doing?
◆ Are areas closed off?
◆ If children are in school, how will they leave safely?

It is very difficult to determine when to scale down or conclude operations following one of these disasters. However, the CCT, with the crisis response team, should announce an **estimated** time of completion with sufficient time for the media to prepare its coverage.

Later, in the **diminishing crisis phase,** address questions, such as:

◆ How many schools have closed?

◆ Which streets are flooded?
◆ Was anybody injured?
◆ How many customers are without electricity, for how long?
◆ Which offices and services are operating, which are closed?

6.7 Human-caused hazards

Typically, this would include terrorism and terrorist hoaxes, hostage-taking, school and workplace violence, civil disturbance, and armed conflict. Human-caused hazard guidelines apply to many different situations to protect rescue efforts, investigations and victims. These incidents can cause potentially harmful psychological effects for the responders, stakeholders and public. See section *7.12 Understanding the psychological effects of a crisis* to shape messages accordingly and with sensitivity.

◆ **Perimeter:** establish a safe distance between the media and the incident scene to maintain responder operations and safety for the press:
  • Issue site-specific media badges listing verified reporter information: name, title, respective editor/producer, contact information
  • Staff post entrances to ensure only authorized media enter
◆ **Media pool:** designate video/photo representatives from responder unit or from the media in order to:
  • Preserve the scene

- Allow emergency responders to conduct operations
- Shield victims from excessive attention
- Economize use of transportation assets
- Protect the media from hazardous materials or other dangers at or near the site
◆ **Sensitive information:** provide all releasable information and explain why officials cannot reveal other information on rescue, recovery, investigative efforts, military campaign or other related matters
◆ **Key messages:** issue short, concise messages regarding empathy, response capabilities and future steps to establish credibility and authority.

Section *6.4 Key messages* explains how to create these messages.

6.7.1 Terrorism or terrorism hoaxes
It is generally recognized that **terrorist organizations seek media coverage of their actions.** Modern terrorism is largely a form of political communication. As ABC's *Nightline* host Ted Koppel once said,

"Without the [media], terrorism becomes rather like the philosopher's tree falling in the forest: no one hears it fall and therefore it has no reason for being."

To complicate matters, acts of terrorism are often seen on-air before the crisis response team and CCT can assemble. Networks air as much footage as possible, to communicate the cause and scope of the unfolding emergency to the authorities and public. Media organizations often release unedited visuals taken by the press, responders or even bystanders. For example, major news networks aired coverage of the attacks on the World Trade Center on September 11, 2001 using footage from private citizens. Some of the impromptu audio included expletives normally edited out of footage, indicating the speed with which the outlets aired the material. The immediate and extensive coverage of television, radio and newspapers serves as a medium for terrorists' propaganda objective: to instill fear.

24-hour news cycle

Since terrorism is a global concern, media organizations around the world devote significant resources to cover all elements of such an incident. **Therefore, organizations need to be able to respond to a surge of media attention to verify information quickly and keep citizens advised of any actions they need to take.**

- ◆ If an attack occurs, maintain staff in communications offices **24 hours per day**
- ◆ Ensure that CCT spokesperson(s) **work in shifts, allowing for sufficient rest**
- ◆ **Regularly update an incident-specific website** to offer background information and chronicle events for worldwide, around-the-clock coverage

Voluntary coverage restraints

Because major media organizations have instituted voluntary terrorism coverage guidelines, CCTs can pursue mutual agreements regarding terror attacks or foiled attempts, including the following real-life examples.

The Radio Telefis Eireann (RTE) Authority in the Republic of Ireland requires that **all interviews with designated groups be pre-recorded and only included in broadcasts if first cleared** by divisional heads, or if necessary, the RTE Director General.

CBS News in the United States uses these terrorism reporting parameters:

◆ **Avoid interference with** the authorities' **communications channels** (for example, tying up telephone lines)
◆ **Use expert advisers** whenever possible, to help avoid questions or reports that might exacerbate the situation
◆ **Observe all emergency services' instructions** – although a provision exists for reporters to report to their superiors if any instructions seem to be intended to suppress the news
◆ **Balance and limit news** coverage to ensure that the (terrorist) story does not unduly crowd out other important broadcasts of the hour or day, domestically and abroad
◆ **Avoid copycat coverage:** prevent offering step-

by-step details of the incident in order to preclude 'copycat' acts. Do not glorify the perpetrator and research problems that led to the event.

Other agreements CCTs can pursue with the press include:

◆ Use key messages to advance the recovery mission and not the terrorist goals
◆ Explain how parents can communicate the issues to their children
◆ Highlight criminal nature of terrorist act(s)
◆ Do not reveal tactics that prevented previous terrorist attempts
◆ Monitor media to correct misinformation as soon as possible
◆ Shield victims and families' members from being interviewed, due to uncertain security situation and possible physical and mental condition(s) related to the incident

Bioterrorism hoax

In April 1997, a suspicious package was found at the Washington, DC offices of B'nai B'rith, an international Jewish organization. The package contained a petri dish labeled 'Anthrax'. Responders from fire/emergency services and the FBI arrived to find several staff in the building complaining of dizziness and headaches.

Thirty people exposed to the element, including civilians, police officers and fire-rescue personnel, were put through decontamination procedures. Police complained when some networks covered the incident live from the top of a nearby building. The live coverage of B'nai B'rith employees showering in the background compromised their privacy making them reluctant to continue the decontamination process.

Senior public affairs officials, including those from the White House and the Federal Emergency Management Agency, did not have a prepared action plan to use the media to relay important information and to solidify the responding agencies' capability to resolve the incident. The lack of a technical spokesperson at the incident effectively forced the media to turn to experts not directly involved for commentary and speculative statements sent conflicting messages to the public.

In the end, mishandling of the press caused more trouble than did the contents of the mysterious package, which turned out to be a hoax.

Source: Bonnie Piper, Deputy Director Media Relations Office of Public Affairs, US Environmental Protection Agency

6.7.2 Hostage-taking
Careful cooperation from the media during a hostage-taking is critical to the safety of the hostages and responders. Hostage-takers usually attempt to contact the media to:

◆　Create panic

◆ Make demands
◆ Obtain sympathy for their cause

Assume the hostage-taker is monitoring media coverage to **obtain information about the hostages** as well as the **authorities' raid-and-rescue mission.**

Ground rules
Communications officers must immediately establish the following ground rules for reporters, producers and editors to promote the success of the rescue operation:

◆ **Geographic perimeter:** specified distance from the scene must be enforced and respected to avoid visuals of responders' tactical positions
◆ **Media role:** discourage the media from taking a role in impromptu negotiations or rescue operations, as any action could affect the mission
◆ **Media calls:** discourage media from calling the hostage-taker or anyone else inside the scene. Media phone calls can compromise a rescue mission by tying up phone lines, tipping off a hostage-taker and in other ways.
◆ **No live coverage:** live coverage could compromise the mission and broadcast inappropriate visuals
◆ **News helicopters:** cannot fly over the scene due to noise and the effect it may have on the actions of hostage-taker (for example, if the hostage-taker believes the helicopter is a part of the raid mission)
◆ **Hostage-taker interaction:** avoid interviewing,

calling or speaking to the hostage-taker. If the hostage-taker calls the media, the reporter should immediately contact the CCT Leader with all of the information.

◆ **Hostages:** do not release information on identity, medical condition, employment, role in community and family members during the incident

◆ **Interviews**
  • **Responders:** for the sake of security and possible negotiations, responders cannot provide mission specifics, including tactics and position and number of responders
  • **Hostages and family members:** during and after the incident, shield these individuals from interviews, due to uncertain security situation and possible physical and mental condition(s)

Source: Bob Steele, 'Crisis Coverage', The Radio and Television News Directors Association, http://www.rtnda.org/ethics/ crisis.shtml, September 19, 2002

6.7.3 School violence
CCTs at educational facilities need to communicate with their stakeholders as quickly as possible due to the sensitive nature of managing child safety.

It is critical that the organization communicate key messages to the following groups:

Students
◆ **Evacuation:** quickly issue clear and calming

instructional messages to direct the students to safety

◆ **Interviews:** discourage students from offering or accepting interviews with the media. Explain that interviews require experience and that if the student accidentally says something he or she regrets, the experience can cause or worsen psychological trauma and aftershock. (Guilt and self-criticism regarding his or her interview can impede the healing process.)

Emergency services

◆ Provide incident information and school map immediately to the responders' CCT for them to coordinate their communications response
◆ Request additional staff to aid in evacuations, communications as needed
◆ Consider setting up a JIC to coordinate actions

Parents

◆ Contact parents at work and home as quickly as possible to notify them of **pertinent safety and schedule information:**
  • School evacuations
  • Pick-up locations
  • Class changes
  • All other details specific to the safety of the children
  • Possible hotline number for parents to call with questions

See *Jane's School Safety Handbook* for further instructions on incident planning, response and recovery procedures.

Ground rules

Educational facilities need to establish **ground rules with the media via a press release to reporters, editors and producers** to ensure the physical and emotional health of children during and after the incident.

◆ **Interviews:** do not interview children, even if they approach reporters
◆ **Copycat coverage:** avoid offering step-by-step details of the incident to preclude students from committing 'copycat' acts. Avoid glorifying the perpetrator and cover problems that led to the event.
◆ **Media pools:** designate media videographers and photographers to obtain visuals for use by participating media organizations. This will limit exposure to children and avoid hindering any response/recovery missions.
◆ **Visual rotation:** avoid repeatedly airing the same tragic visuals, so that students can start the healing process

Source: 'Crisis Communications Tool and Guide Kit,' The National Education Association, http://www.nea.org/crisis, April 22, 2002

School shooting

On April 20, 1999, two students at Columbine High School in Colorado killed 10 fellow students and one teacher, and injured 24 others before killing themselves.

Jefferson County's Public Schools Communications Services responded to the tragedy including over 2,000 media queries and charitable offers. Working out of its on-site communications center, every day this unit formulated key messages with legal and management teams; provided talking points for school district spokespeople; held two press conferences; arranged individual interviews and put out news releases and fact sheets for state and nationwide distribution. Every week, the team sent talking points to 143 other schools for staff and parents. To inject positive images into the news coverage, the team created a tribute web page and a video tape. A hotline took in offers of monetary and material assistance from around the world.

In the recognition phase of the crisis, the team coordinated memorial services, VIP visits, tours of the reconstructed school and media coverage of the day classes resumed. Finally, the team developed a post-incident multimedia training presentation for school district officials, emergency responders and law enforcement officers.

Source: 'The Columbine Tragedy: Managing the Unthinkable,' 2000 Silver Anvil Award for Crisis Management, http:// www.prsa.org/Awards/silver/html/6BW0011B02.html

6.7.4 Civil disturbance

Civil disturbances may be organized public protests with advanced notice to authorities or may occur spontaneously in reaction to an upsetting event. Either way, violence, vandalism and/or looting can result. The following entities may consider forming a JIC to create cohesive messages to calm the public:

◆ State/province governor's office
◆ City mayor's office
◆ Police department
◆ Fire department
◆ Other emergency services: medical, bomb, hazardous materials (HAZMAT)
◆ School districts

During the incident, **do not place blame on one group or another to avoid inciting further disruption.** Wait until all information is available and analyzed before confronting the community with responsibility.

Ground rules

Response organizations need to work with the media on measuring the coverage to preclude any injuries and loss of life or property. Request the following:

◆ Avoid repeatedly airing images of violent acts that may encourage similar acts, mischaracterize level of disturbance or exacerbate socio-economic divisions

◆ Limit helicopter coverage, so as not to increase the sense of disorder

◆ Do not report locations that are vulnerable due to limited police presence

---

Civil disturbance coverage

Media coverage of the police beating of Rodney King played a role in the 1992 Los Angeles riots. The repeated airing of the citizen-recorded videotape of the incident reinforced grievances toward the police in South Central Los Angeles. In turn, news of the acquittal of the four police officers involved set off rioting.

Local television broadcasts of the looting contributed to others joining in. The television helicopters reported on areas lacking police presence, effectively directing the looters to vulnerable areas. Another citizen recording of the beating of bystander Reginald Denny also seared into the public's psyche. Reporting in the *Los Angeles Times* had been more restrained than television coverage, but both broadcast and print media engaged in controversial and sensationalized reporting. Such coverage is believed to have led to related civil disturbances in Las Vegas, Seattle and San Francisco.

Los Angeles Mayor Tom Bradley's request on the second day to stop publicizing violent images to one television station came too late to stop the five days of rioting. The cost amounted to 50 people dead,

---

thousands injured and US$1billion in property damages.

Source: 'Media Interaction with the Public in Emergency Situations: Four Case Studies', A report prepared under an Interagency agreement by the Federal Research Division, Library of Congress, Washington, DC 1999

6.7.5 Workplace violence

Workplace violence is one of the most significant yet least-recognized problems facing many organizations. The US National Crime Victimization Survey reported that an average of 1.7 million violent acts were committed against individuals at work or on duty per year from 1993 to 1999. The US National Institute of Occupational Safety and Health (NIOSH) estimates the economic cost of workplace violence at around US$121 billion per year.

Background information

The CCT must be aware of the organizations' operations policies and procedures, especially when it may need to respond to questions regarding prevention and training. See section *3.4.1 Approval process to release information* for further guidance on commenting on regular internal operations.

Ground rules

Private organizations have often been publicly criticized for withholding important information out of self-interest. Although protection of business classified information is permissible, see guidance on 'ground rules' from the following sections to exercise privacy rights within limits:

Section *6.7.1 Terrorism or terrorism hoaxes*
Section *6.7.2 Hostage-taking*
Section *6.7.3 School violence*
Section *6.7.4 Civil disturbance*

6.7.6 War and conflict
Be prepared to operate communications offices 24 hours per day to report developments. This schedule will also need to respond externally to the around-the-clock domestic and international media presence.

Military communications officers need to be conscious of timely clearance of information once an operation is complete, at which point the officer can expand on details previously judged operationally sensitive. If information is inadvertently released through unauthorized disclosure or possibly existing, indirect channels; be prepared to comment using **key messages.** See section *6.4 Key messages* for guidance on creating appropriate capabilities responses.

Organize any declassified information from completed operations to inform the public on the status of war campaigns:

◆   Location

◆ Force capabilities: mountain, air, sea, desert, special missions
◆ Duration
◆ Casualties
◆ Number of troops
◆ Type and number of weapons, bombs used
◆ Number of missions
◆ Nature of new technologies, if not still classified

Media access
◆ **Perimeter:** establish a distance from the operations scene for the media to maintain operations and safety for the press
  • Issue media badges specific to the site according to confirmed reporter information: name, title, respective editor/producer, contact information
  • Staff entrance posts to ensure only authorized media enter
◆ **Media pool:** designate video/photo representatives from unit or from the media in order to:
  • Conduct operations
  • Accommodate for space constraints on travel to the site
  • Protect the media from hazardous materials or action, at or near the site
◆ **Sensitive information:** explain why officials cannot reveal information on parts of operations

Conflict areas abroad

These incidents may involve coups, uprisings or terrorism in urban or rural areas. These events may require military, diplomatic and/or humanitarian responses. CCTs from those areas need to be aware of the security implications of the release of information on their operations on websites, pamphlets or in local papers:

◆ Identity and titles of employees and family members
◆ Supplies stored in facilities: medical equipment/ pharmaceuticals, technology (computers, phones, fax machines), emergency food/water, weapons
◆ Security provisions: ensure surveillance/recording equipment are not pronounced on outside fixtures

Also, carefully limit staff access to potentially sensitive information. This staff may include: security guards, translators, cooks, cleaners and administrative staff.

6.8 Mechanical/technological malfunction

These incidents may include product or operational failures or accidents in areas such as transportation, infrastructure and/or facilities. Research the following information to determine course of action and recovery requirements.

Incident details

◆ Have regulatory/enforcement agencies contacted the organization?
◆ What events led to the incident?

◆ Were employees or bystanders involved?
  • Were those involved authorized to be on the premises during the event?
  • What were they doing before and at the time of the event?
◆ What should the public know to avoid further loss/damage?

Previous incident-related history/preparedness
◆ Have such incidents occurred at the organization in the past?
◆ What is the record in the area of operation affected, such as security, safety and regulatory approvals/inspections?

Possible losses
◆ What is the estimated financial loss from damage to a facility?
◆ What type of insurance coverage did the organization have?
◆ What is the impact on customers and what recourse do they have?

Background information
The CCT must be aware of the organization's operations policies and procedures, especially when it may need to answer or decline questions regarding prevention and training. See section *3.4.1 Approval process to release information* for further guidance on commenting on regular internal operations.

Response in an isolated area

The 1996 ValuJet airplane crash in the isolated Florida Everglades presented operational and communications response challenges. Only helicopters and airboats could reach the area leaving the majority of the responders 300 yards away. The fire rescue public information officer (PIO) on-scene could not activate his team due to an overwhelmed cellular network. Government offices closed for the weekend and their subsequent differing media policies challenged inter-agency cooperation.

Nevertheless, the PIO who arrived within an hour of the crash established a media staging area, held a briefing within 15 minutes and conducted subsequent briefings every 30 minutes for the next 10 hours. The incident commander and the first rescuer on-scene provided evening interviews and sound bites for nightly and next morning news programs. A PIO liaison also worked inside the Joint Operations Command post to coordinate with the rescue effort and collect information for release.

When no survivors of the 110 passengers were found, they announced the victim recovery/identification would transition into an investigation led by the National Transportation Safety Board (NTSB). Although a new briefing schedule and media site was set up at a local hotel, the recovery team on-scene commitment lasted

30 days. Throughout, they continued to provide sound bites as well as pool video and photography of the site.

Lessons learned: quick communications response critically established the efficient flow of information to the public via the media. Communications teams must prepare for long operations and environmental effects on personnel and equipment.

6.9 Communications deliverables

Upon reaching agreement on the approach and key messages for a specific incident type, various team members should begin developing the materials based on a comprehensive list of communications deliverables specific to the sector.

See *Chapter 7: Engaging Key Stakeholders* for procedures on creating deliverables for affected groups. See *Chapter 8: Working with the Media* to respond to press inquires and communicate to the general public. Lastly, see section *10.1 Response procedures check lists* for clearance procedures to distribute those materials quickly according to the rollout plan.

CHAPTER 7: ENGAGING KEY STAKEHOLDERS

CHAPTER 7: ENGAGING KEY STAKEHOLDERS

7.1 Introduction

The Crisis Communications Team (CCT) must engage the organization's supporters and other groups the emergency affects in order to resolve crises quickly and maintain its credibility. This chapter will discuss how to **create specific key messages and to understand the psychological impact** on stakeholders potentially involved:

◆ Victims and families
◆ Employees
◆ Community where event occurred and/or where the organization operates
◆ Customers
◆ Investors
◆ Government: enforcement, regulators and elected officials

7.2 Benefits of interacting with stakeholders

By **speaking and listening** to groups and individuals the crisis affects, the organization can increase the likelihood of the following:

◆ **Establish authority** and capability to end the crisis
◆ **Disseminate information** not appropriate for press coverage (such as sensitive information for victims and families)

◆ **Confirm facts,** control rumors
◆ **Ensure public safety** (such as directing affected people to take health-related actions)
◆ **Identify the organization** with involved/affected individuals
◆ **Acknowledge concerns** of those affected
◆ **Better understand** the nature of the emergency
◆ **Mitigate further damage**
◆ **Continue operations** for future service
◆ **Avoid negative outcomes:** loss of public/financial support, investigation of poor response
◆ **Develop a call to action:** involve the audience in the response effort and allow the public to feel a sense of control. In some cases, establish a toll-free number or announce a website for the public to provide information or share concerns.

Psychological aspects of a crisis

Often, crises result in varying and complex psychological phenomena. For example, common experiences among the 5,300 individuals exposed to nerve gas in the 1995 attack on Kasumigaseki Station in the Tokyo subway system included anxiety, fear, nightmares, insomnia, depression and fear of subways. These reactions and others often surprised and alarmed the victims. By recognizing and acknowledging a range of emotions, the organization supports victims' needs for help and for coping resources. The US Centers for Disease Control and Prevention (CDC) have conducted and compiled research on how crisis responders can better communicate – and address their own coping – by understanding these psychological responses. Incorporating instructions or messages with an understanding of these conditions can greatly augment a communications strategy and/or be used with accompanying fact sheets.

Oklahoma City bombing

Two years after the Oklahoma City bombing, 16 percent of children and adolescents who lived approximately 100 miles from Oklahoma City reported significant Post-traumatic Stress Disorder (PTSD) symptoms related to the event. PTSD occurs when the physical and emotional responses to a traumatic event continue to affect people after the danger has passed. This is an important finding because these youths were not directly exposed to the trauma and were not related to victims who had been killed or injured. PTSD symptoms were greater in those with more media exposure and in those with indirect interpersonal exposure, such as having a friend who knew someone who was killed or injured.

Source: B. Pfefferbaum, R. Gurwitch, N. McDonald, M. Leftwich, G. Sconzo, A. Messenbaugh, and R. Schultz. 'Posttraumatic Stress among Children after the Death of a Friend or Acquaintance in a Terrorist Bombing,' Psychiatric Services, 51, 2000, 386-388.

Media coverage

The media's tone, message repetition and choice of

imagery may also increase or cause negative emotional responses for the involved parties and even the general viewing audience. In turn, the CCT should distribute its own video/photography of the incident, capturing images of dedication to recovery efforts and any rescue successes. The CCT should also work with the media to cover positive 'milestone' events.

Honeymoon period

Although a crisis may involve negative consequences on many levels, positive outcomes are possible, which an organization can use to galvanize support to resolve the crisis. The swift response in the United States and around the world to attacks in New York City, Washington, DC and Pennsylvania is one example.

The **'honeymoon period'** following an emergency may include stakeholder support, such as:

◆ Resilience and coping
◆ Altruism
◆ Relief and elation at surviving the disaster
◆ Sense of excitement and greater self-worth
◆ Changes in the way the future is viewed
◆ Feelings of strength and growth from the experience

If applicable, see section *7.12 Understanding the psychological effects of a crisis* for further research from the CDC on the mental and emotional impact of emergencies.

CHAPTER 7: Engaging Key Stakeholders   www.janes.com

7.3 Stakeholder groups

While different groups may have varying connections to a crisis and/or the organization(s) involved, some groups have similar information needs. For emergencies involving public safety issues, see the figure 7.1 for a diagram on the relationships among the parties involved.

Figure 7.1 Audience Relationships

*Source: <u>CDC Crisis and Emergency Risk Communications,</u>
September 2002*

7.4 Key messages

Key messages to stakeholders must be consistent with messages delivered to the media for the general public. Stakeholder messages, however, may include extra information or instructions, such as a need for employees to provide additional assistance or change work routines. In all cases, the organization's message must express:

◆ Dedication to resolving or mitigating the crisis
◆ Commitment to quick action
◆ Intent to inform stakeholders
◆ Provision of resources that provide healing, comfort and empowerment

7.5 Information to victims and families

The **first priority** of an organization responding to an emergency should be to **provide notification to family members and coordinate family briefings prior to releasing victims' names to the public.** Family members should then be given time to notify other family members and friends, prior to public release of the victims' names. Organizations do not want to increase the pain the event may cause to these people by having them learn of important event details through the media – particularly the identification of victims or details of how victims were killed or injured.

Consider the following provisions the US National Transportation Safety Board has established to protect families of airplane-accident victims:

◆ **Hotel:** to ensure privacy, designate a single hotel for victims and families, separated from any establishment the organization uses for its Crisis Center. Issue identification cards for family members. (Reporters have occasionally misrepresented themselves as family members to obtain access and interview family members.)

◆ **Security guards:** if necessary, provide staff to prohibit the media from unauthorized entry into the families' hotel

◆ **Information phone lines:** provide family members with a **private**, toll-free number that gives information on victim identification, recovery efforts and healing/coping assistance

◆ **General assistance:** provide information on response and recovery efforts by local authorities, such as points of contact for criminal investigations, hospitals and the medical examiner

◆ **Memorial services:** hold them near the incident scene and allow family members to visit. (A media pool may be established to provide coverage.)

◆ **Briefing with involved organizations:** conduct a briefing for representatives of other organizations to describe and/or coordinate the assistance provided to the families

Communicating to grieving families

The tragic 1996 crash of TWA Flight 800 was a watershed event for the US Coast Guard (USCG) because it firmly established the need to communicate effectively with the 230 victims' families. Chief Public Affairs Officer CDR James McPherson moved between media briefings in Moriches, NY and the hotel at JFK airport, where the 600 families were meeting along with TWA staff. CDR McPherson, with USCG family liaison and search and rescue officers, would show the families charts and photos of each day's search area and answer questions. "It was certainly the most difficult and emotional public affairs challenge I ever faced," he said.

These briefings brought great comfort to the families. The most important step was for a senior USCG official to inform the families first and privately when the search was suspended. The hundreds of the families grieved in different ways, and it was an emotional event for all the participants, including the federal, state and local first responders. Some of the families were in shock, some were in denial and some were very angry. In the end, however, all the families understood that the federal government did everything it could. After this incident, the USCG formalized plans to have a continuous flow of information to the families during such incidents.

Source: CDR James McPherson, Chief, Media Relations, US Coast Guard

Because a communications officer is the liaison

between the press and the organization for interviews and press conferences, he or she can make arrangements when a victim or family member **wants to speak** with media. Work with the press to obtain as many interview details as possible. See section *8.6.3 Interview guidelines* for interview do's and do not's and additional guidance.

7.6 Employee communications

During crises, employee communications are just as important as communications to external stakeholders. Timely and direct communication with employees is crucial for a number of reasons:

◆ Employees will inevitably be concerned about their organization, families and community. As a rule, **they would much rather hear any important news from their employer than from the press.**

◆ **Inviting outside experts,** such as officials from emergency response or research specialists, to explain risks or give instructions to employees will establish the organization's ability to mitigate related problems.

◆ Ultimately, **employees are messengers for an organization.** If they have the right information, they can play a role in shaping perceptions throughout the community. In acting as 'ambassadors' for the organization in the larger community, employees may express the positive feelings associated with the 'honeymoon' period following a crisis.

7.6.1 Employee communications vehicles
There are several options to communicate with employees about a crisis situation.

◆ **Employee meetings:** face-to-face or small group meetings are often the best way to communicate in a crisis situation, especially since they provide two-way communication

◆ **E-mail:** while e-mail is perhaps the quickest way to disseminate news, it is important to ensure that everyone the organization needs to reach has access to the system and regularly reads his or her e-mail. Keep in mind that because e-mail is easily forwarded and internal communications are likely to become public quickly.

◆ **Bulletin board/intranet announcements:** in organizations where employees are accustomed to reading bulletin boards or checking an intranet site for announcements, both venues can provide an effective way to disseminate information quickly

◆ **Teleconferences:** this method enables a large number of employees to hear directly from a senior executive; it is particularly useful in the case of a large, geographically diverse employee base

◆ **Letters and memos:** this is a useful vehicle, especially if there are additional materials, such as frequently asked questions, that the organization wants to distribute to employees. One way to draw special attention to urgent news is to print the letter on colored paper.

◆ **Toll-free phone line:** a toll-free number that provides a 'human voice' serves as another way for employees to speak with someone directly if they have questions or concerns. These telephone numbers can be included in letters sent to employees.

◆ **Video and slide presentations:** both tools offer another way to provide additional information to employees as well as to reinforce messages previously communicated in a meeting. However, since it takes time to develop these presentations, they are generally most useful as **post-incident communications or in continuing situations.**

7.7 Community communications

An organization can communicate with its community indirectly through the community's neighborhood associations, elected leadership, local media and an organization's own employees, who often live in an employer's community. However, it is sometimes advisable, depending on the nature and severity of the crisis situation, for an organization to communicate directly and **proactively** with the community itself. Some methods include:

◆ Placing advertising, such as an open letter to the community, in the local newspaper
◆ Identifying and reaching out to the informal opinion leaders of the community, such as business, education and/or religious leaders
◆ Mailing an open letter to the community

◆ Holding a town meeting or open house
◆ Creating a crisis response page on the organization's website with background, response, coping and contact information.

7.8 Investment community communications

In crisis situations affecting public companies, it may be necessary to communicate directly with the investment community. Such proactive communications are required if an event, or the implications of an event, are deemed to have a potential impact on the company. In addition, some situations not legally 'material' to the company may require proactive communications in order to mitigate potential concerns.

Proactive techniques include: distributing public statements/releases to the investment community and the media, holding one-on-one phone calls and hosting an open conference call for the investment community. In the case of a public company, care must be given to ensure the company adheres to financial regulations, such as those of the US Securities and Exchange Commission, and does not selectively disclose material information.

There may be some cases where proactive outreach to the investment community is unnecessary. However, in all situations, the company's investor relations professionals and/or senior management should be prepared to respond to inquiries.

Credibility restored

Based on strong sales and growth prospects, the children's apparel company, The Children's Place, conducted its initial public offering in September 1997, at US$14 per share. The unpredictable warm weather and some merchandising missteps caused an unexpected drop in sales and a stock price fall to US$4. Analysts abandoned the stock and a group of investors claimed the sales prospects were misleading. Company research revealed the weak sales season was isolated. Also, its unique merchandising strategy and a strong brand image validated its growth plans.

To restore its credibility, the company engaged existing and potential investors, analysts and the financial and industry media. By conducting and following-up on meetings with investors and store tours with analysts, the company improved its financial image. Following two consecutive earnings periods of excellent sales/ earnings growth, it marked its revival with a 'Back to School' analyst/financial media fashion presentation during autumn 1998. Building relationships with retail reporters resulted in coverage of their sales success and attracted financial media, analysts and portfolio managers to this event. The company was able to showcase its solid merchandising and sales trends, strong brand appeal and its price-to-value fashions. Consequently, the stock appreciated to US$30 per share.

Source: 'The Children's Place with Morgen-Walke Associates',
Silver Anvil Awards, http://www.prsa.org/_Awards/silver/ html/6BW9913A.html

7.9 Customer communications

While customers may learn of an organization's crisis through media coverage or other means, the organization should also plan for direct communications to customers. A few vehicles include:

◆ **Direct telephone calls:** in severe situations it may be appropriate to place calls to major customers
◆ **Direct mail/e-mail:** direct mail, in the form of e-mail, faxed or posted letters and so on can reach a broader group of customers
◆ **Specialist call center:** vendors can provide call banks with operators who can handle a heavy call load and provide live or recorded information to customers. An organization can also set up a toll-free number for customer assistance.

7.10 Government communications
Regulatory/Law Enforcement

Most often, crises will result in the involvement of investigative, enforcement and/or regulatory authorities. Frequently, the authorities involved will direct how communications about the actual incident and/or investigation are handled, especially when public safety issues or investigations in involved. The organization should:

◆ Comply with the authorities' requests/instructions
◆ Be sensitive to the authorities' concerns

◆ Ensure that Joint Information Center (JIC) with authorities serves the general public interest rather than the organization's private interests
◆ Communicate the organization's own key messages about its actions, efforts and priorities using forum separate from the JIC

Oil tanker spill

The US Coast Guard (USCG) needed to spend a great deal of time discussing who was in charge of the JIC at a major oil spill because a private company attempted to use the JIC credibility to put out inaccurate information favorable to the company. The representative from the oil company attempted to change the information the JIC was going to release to indicate that the source of the thousands of gallons of spilled oil was not yet determined. The USCG confirmed immediately that the 20-foot hole in their oil tanker was the source. The oil company's behavior thus threatened the accuracy of the information to the public, its credibility for possible investigations and further dealings with the authorities.

Source: CDR James McPherson, Chief, Media Relations, US Coast Guard

---

Elected officials

In many crises, communications with federal, state or local government elected officials are critical. Keeping elected officials briefed on the situation can help minimize public criticism and acquire additional

---

resources. Public officials generally garner significant press attention in crisis situations and can help communicate an organization's message with the added credibility their office provides.

Guidelines in communicating with elected officials include:

◆ Provide timely responses to all government inquiries. Track correspondence to establish who handled the query and the turnaround time.
◆ Communicate the organization's complete cooperation with the authorities/investigating agencies
◆ When possible and appropriate, refer to the organization's track record of responsible behavior in all operations
◆ Avoid any activity with elected officials that may seem inappropriate. A political scandal will cause significant damage to the organization and the official in question.

Overall, organizations need to engage all involved groups during a crisis and not just the ones seemingly most important. The following case study is an example of how to engage all involved groups.

Strategic turnaround

"Can George Fisher Fix Kodak?" asked the October 20, 1997, cover story of *Business Week*. Eastman Kodak Company, led by Chief Executive Officer George Fisher, experienced losses in revenue and earnings growth from poor returns on digital imaging investments, increased competition and the Asian financial crisis. Management had to take immediate and bold response steps while restoring public confidence.

Kodak announced their plans including: job reductions and other tough restructuring steps, a growth strategy in China and strategic alliances with AOL and Intel during 1997 and early 1998. The executive team communicated regularly to employees with letters, intranet communications, videos and meetings to explain the company's growth plan. External communications consisted of updating the media on strategies to reach customers, meeting with major investors in the US and Europe and speaking to community leaders and elected officials at the local, state and federal levels.

As a result, the company gained consumer interest and market share. Surveys showed employee satisfaction increased. Investors, community leaders and elected officials appreciated access to management, its disclosure and commitment to the community. *Business Week* thus reported on July 27, 1998, "At last, a Bright Kodak Moment."

Source: 'Kodak Company with Shandwick', Silver Anvil Awards, http://www.prsa.org/_Awards/silver/html/6BW9902A.html

---

7.11 Managing volunteer and charitable offers
Often the CCT will be entrusted with facilitating incoming volunteer and charitable assistance during and after a crisis.

◆ Designate person(s) to manage the operation
◆ Designate a sector or staging area for incoming volunteer and charitable offers
◆ Follow up with letters of appreciation

Volunteer or charitable offers can significantly help – but also divert – CCT attention away from executing the crisis communication plan. If the organization has a relationship with other entities accustomed or familiar with handling this type of situation, such as the Red Cross or local charitable organizations, request they manage the volunteer and charitable offers.

7.12 Understanding the psychological effects of a crisis
If the incident involves a severe impact on the organization, community and/or stakeholders; it is important to understand the psychological impact on all of those audiences when creating messages with empathy and understanding. It is also important to understand that even the media coverage can have a long-term physical and emotional impact on those affected groups and the public. **This reinforces the need for media ground rules to protect the well-being of victims, witnesses and others the media might want to interview.**

7.12.1 Emotional Responses

Emotional responses to traumatic incidents include but are not limited to the areas in the following chart. Some of these reactions can **unnecessarily tax the response and CCT efforts to engage with stakeholders.**

Thoughts	Reactions
Vicarious Rehearsal	Observers visualize own involvement Consider effect of response on them Reject response plan and offer another Falsely feel at risk and desire attention
Denial	Ignore warnings Find the warning confusing Refuse to believe threat or effect
Stigmatization	Community refuses services or access Community diminishes risks to a group
Fear/Avoidance	Act personally to avoid a threat Irrational and danger to others
Withdrawal/ Hopelessness/ Helplessness	Feel powerless Lack effort for precautionary action May ignore messages to evacuate

7.12.2 Harmful actions

The negative emotions commonly experienced in a crisis or disaster – **left without mitigating communication from a trusted source** – may lead to harmful individual or group behaviors. Those behaviors can hamper response and recovery efforts or even create new crises.

◆ **Misallocation** of attention and/or treatments
◆ **Boycotting or protesting** a company or product
◆ **Special attention** requests (or accusations) for individual considerations based on connections
◆ **Fraud** due to special circumstances
◆ **Creating false information** about people/products
◆ **Distrust** of government or company
◆ **Bribery** for scarce treatments and/or resources

Self-destructive behaviors among adults as reactions to stress may include:

◆ Increased alcohol and tobacco use
◆ Inattention to family and work responsibilities
◆ Depression and anxiety
◆ In emergencies involving a biological disease, a phenomenon known as **Multiple Unexplained Physical Symptoms (MUPS)** could confound the effort to identify those people who need immediate care versus those who need limited treatments or pharmaceuticals

7.12.3 Traumatic stress disorder

Traumatic stress overwhelms coping mechanisms and may produce a sense of helplessness and loss of control. It is not uncommon for individuals exposed to traumatic events – **including victims, the responders and the CCT** – to exhibit a wide array of thoughts, feelings and behavior during and after a traumatic event. Some of these characteristics are listed in the following table. **Note: this is not an all-inclusive list, nor does the presence of a symptom within this list imply specific medical diagnoses.** When in doubt, consult a physician. When communicating to groups individually or as a whole, be aware of these possible conditions.

Reactions	Symptoms	
Cognitive	Confusion Poor problem-solving Difficulty calculating Heightened anxiety Memory impairment	Distractibility Inattention Disorientation Lowered alertness Poor judgment
Physical	Rapid heart rate Tremors Intestinal upset Nausea Sleep disturbance Elevated blood pressure	Chills Dizziness Chest pains Headaches Fatigue
Behavioral	Difficulty sleeping Appetite change Startle response Isolation Fatigue	Nightmares Hyper-vigilance Withdrawal Avoidance Substance abuse
Emotional	Guilt Fear Shock Sadness Irritability	Anger Anxiety Disbelief Hopelessness Numbness
Grief process	Shock/denial Anger Acceptance	Bargaining Depression

7.12.4 Post-Traumatic Stress Disorder (PTSD)

PTSD occurs when the physical and emotional responses to a traumatic event continue to affect people after the danger has passed. A person with PTSD can be debilitated by feelings of panic and recurring symptoms for months, even years. The majority of traumatized individuals do not develop PTSD. The frequency of PTSD cases varies from about 4 to 30 percent. The following characterizes the symptoms, most common incident causes and resulting disorders:

Symptoms
◆ Exposure to a traumatic stressor
◆ Recurrent symptoms of traumatic stress
◆ Avoidance responses and emotional numbness
◆ Increased arousal/anxiety
◆ Duration of at least one month
◆ Significant distress or impairment of functioning

Related incidents
◆ Exposure to mass destruction or death
◆ Toxic contamination
◆ Sudden or violent death of a loved one
◆ Loss of home or community

Associated disorders
◆ Depression
◆ Substance abuse
◆ Panic disorder

◆ Obsessive-compulsive disorder
◆ Sexual dysfunction
◆ Eating disorders

7.12.5 Understanding issues of death, dying and grief

People communicating to an individual or community experiencing loss of life must be especially aware of the grief process. Grief is experienced in a broad social context. Communities may face what experts call **'death out of time,'** or the death of someone who is not advanced in age and/or ill. The death of a child can be much harder to cope with than the death of an adult.

Several factors influence the grief process:

◆ Circumstances of the death
◆ Nature of the relationship with the deceased
◆ Individuals experiencing a prior or multiple losses
◆ Secondary losses, such as isolation from current social groups or loss of ambitions
◆ Proximity to the incident

Grief is a universal emotion, but no two people experience grief in exactly the same manner. Not everyone goes through all of the following stages and some of the stages may overlap:

◆ **Shock and denial:** feelings of disbelief that someone has died or is about to die. These thoughts protect against from the full effect of the news before a person is fully prepared for acceptance.

◆ **Anger:** after acknowledging the reality of a loss, feelings of anger may arise. People may displace pain and place blame on others around them or even on the deceased.

◆ **Bargaining:** even with little or no hope for a recovery, people may tell themselves that they can do something to solve the problem

◆ **Guilt:** feelings of regret or responsibility from past incidents may fosters the belief that one can still change the situation

◆ **Depression:** suddenly or gradually, sadness and crying occurs as the bereaved begins to understand that life needs to continue without the person

◆ **Acceptance:** the final stage, the person accepts the loss. The person may feel forgiveness and a sense of peace about what happened for the first time. The person may still feel sad, but has stopped trying to fight reality. People often start to find an enduring way to pay tribute to the life of the person who has died.

Sources: CDC Crisis and Emergency Risk Communications, September 2002

Lifeworks, 'Coping with Loss and Grief' http://www.lifeworks.com/ctim/index.cfm?ctim=5.46.158.2021

CHAPTER 8: WORKING WITH THE MEDIA

8.1 Introduction

From the onset of an emergency, it is critical to articulate and repeat key messages and respond to media inquiries. **While the organization cannot control what the press reports, the Crisis Communications Team's (CCT) efforts to keep the media informed will encourage the press to regard the organization as the first source of news.** If an organization does not provide the information, the media will be forced to use alternative sources that may not have access to the facts. When making public announcements about an incident, the CCT should have already or simultaneously implemented the procedures listed in *Chapter 5: Gathering and Verifying Information*, *Chapter 6: Messages and Strategy* and *Chapter 7: Engaging Key Stakeholders*. These procedures include: verifying the information, assessing the situation, implementing a strategy and interacting with key stakeholders.

While an organization's response to media inquiries will depend on the type and seriousness of the incident, interacting with the media should ideally include the following steps outlined in this chapter:

(1) Maintaining media logs and monitoring coverage
(2) Issuing a press release
(3) Conducting initial interviews on-phone and/or on-air

(4) Setting up a press conference area and holding a press conference
(5) Organizing additional interviews
(6) Understanding interview formats and do's and do not's

8.2 Media log

Organizations should keep a detailed record of media inquiries. During a crisis, the designated media contact(s), mainly the CCT Leader, will undoubtedly be inundated with calls. A log is instrumental to track those inquiries, to provide a sense of media interest and to indicate the direction future coverage may take. Ensure that support staff members:

◆ Are available to answer phones
◆ Are equipped with a media log
◆ Know to obtain all information listed on the log form
◆ Remember to assure the press that a response is forthcoming
◆ Possess the contact information (cell phone preferably) for the CCT Leader and any potential spokespersons
◆ Know the schedule and whereabouts of the CCT Leader

Interview details checklist

Obtain pertinent details of the interview request to confirm that the proposed interviewee would be the most appropriate spokesperson:

◆ Nature of the interview
◆ Media organization's broadcast area, circulation
◆ Location: if the spokesperson's schedule is extremely busy, request conducting the interview at the office or the site
◆ Potential questions – in order to prepare most effectively
◆ Names and affiliations of additional commentators or experts included in the session
◆ Duration of interview versus actual on-air time or print space/word count – in order to assess how to use key messages most effectively
◆ Whether questions from callers or studio a audience will be taken; from where the people will call

---

See section *8.6.3 Interview guidelines: do's and do not's* to prepare for interviews.

Media log template

Date:			Time:		
Organization name:					
Type of media (circle): wire	print	TV	radio		Internet
Reporter name:					
Producer/editor name:					
Tel:					
Fax:					
E-mail:					
Deadline:					
Interview (circle): live	taped	call-in	on-site		in-studio
Interview times/dates:					
Inquiry details:					
Responded to call: Date:			Time:		

Also see section *10.2 Templates.*

For large numbers of similar questions, **send a common answer by e-mail or fax to the media outlets** simultaneously to avoid returning multiple calls.

8.3 Media monitoring

From the outset, it is vital to monitor all media outlets – wire, print, television, Internet, radio – for coverage. Identifying possible sources of relevant information beforehand should allow the CCT to monitor immediate crisis coverage easily. Although the Internet is a great way to monitor news sources, planning is essential as some news websites only allow on-line access by paid subscription. Having a television with cable access to the major news stations is also very helpful. If a television is in the command center – or where ever the entire crisis response team is working – make sure the television is on mute, ideally with captions, to reduce the noise level and minimize distractions.

A thorough review of media coverage can assist in:

◆ Making real-time correction of mistakes
◆ Identifying areas of interest, bias and spin
◆ Determining how the CCT Leader and other crisis managers can better serve the public
◆ Determining future communications strategy
◆ Learning of events and establishing a chronology for future reference

8.3.1 Making corrections
Organization corrections

If the organization communicates incorrect information, admit responsibility and express regret. It is acceptable to correct a previous action or announcement by issuing a short and concise written press release or statement. It is also acceptable to indicate that the release will be the only statement on the correction. A prolonged press conference and interview process to correct the information tends to distort the message rather than clarify it.

2000 US presidential election

At 7:50 pm EST on Election Night 2000, American television networks projected Democratic candidate Al Gore as the winner of Florida and therefore the likely winner of the presidency. With some Florida polls still open, this announcement violated a commitment to avoid declaring a winner of a state while that state's residents were still voting.

At 10:00 pm, with more votes counted and the totals beginning to swing in Republican George W Bush's favor, the networks rescinded their first projections. At 2:18 am, the networks proclaimed Bush the winner in Florida and the nation's 43rd president. Gore conceded. Many newspapers, already well beyond deadline, started press runs saying Bush had won.

Later, however, the vote totals swung back toward Gore, who around 3:30 am retracted his concession. The networks were appalled. "That would be something, if the networks managed to blow it twice in one night," NBC's Tom Brokaw said on the air.

At 4:00 am, the networks withdrew their prediction of a Bush victory. In the space of eight hours, the presidency of the US, according to the television networks, had gone from Gore to Bush and finally to undecided. The reasons: bad data, competitive pressure and a rush to judgment.

Media corrections

If an error in fact or interpretation has been made, the CCT Leader should discuss the issue personally and affirmatively with the reporter. Many members of the media are thin-skinned about criticism. Therefore, in making corrections do not single out errant reporters publicly, especially during public briefings.

A published correction is justified if an error of fact has been printed. Because of the quick-moving nature of information during crises and reporters' schedules, decide if the fact in question is important enough to insist on a correction.

◆ **Minor error:** an incorrect report that does not misreport the nature of the event. Example: at a press conference, the spokesperson mentioned that 86 fire rescue people participated in the operation, but that morning's paper reported the number as 85.

- **Recourse:** bring the error to the reporter's attention and ask him or her to change the figure in the next article

◆ **Major error:** incorrectly states the course of events or grossly misquotes an individual. Example: if that morning's paper reported that 86 rescue people were fired from their jobs instead of participating in the operation, pursue a formal printed correction.

- **First recourse:** request a correction to be printed in the next issue
- **Second recourse:** If the reporter refuses to print a correction, contact the respective editor

◆ **Widespread error:** the mistaken information is widely disseminated

- **Recourse:** correct it during a public briefing without publicly criticizing the individuals responsible for the mistake.

◆ **Interpretation error:** a report characterizing an event from a different point of view than the organization's. A published **correction will not occur** in most cases.

- **Recourse:** describe to the reporter the organization's point of view and why the difference is important for the recovery operations and public knowledge. This action may allow the organization's interpretation to prevail in subsequent stories.

Pursuing corrections

Within five minutes of a small earthquake in San Jose, California, the local newspaper's reporter phoned and received comment from the Director of Emergency Preparedness, Frances Edwards-Winslow: "That wasn't much of a quake, but we got a pretty good shake. Oh, sorry, I just realized that rhymes." He said he liked the quote and thanked her.

He quoted her as saying, "It was a slam, bam, thank you ma'am kind of quake." Horrified and mortified, she immediately contacted him. The reporter apologized but refused to run a correction since the incident was a 'one day wonder'. The City of San Jose's new public outreach manager made a second request with the editor. He told the PIO it would be worse to make an issue of it as it was a short quote in a longer piece.

Every Sunday, the paper features five or six *Quotes of the Week* at the top of the editorial comment page. The lead quote in the headline was the "slam, bam" statement, attributed to Edwards-Winslow. The result: she never spoke to the reporter again and referred him to the PIO when he called for later stories. Thus, when a breakdown in source-media cooperation occurs, the flow of information slows or even stops. Information providers desire accuracy just as much as the reporters and access for the media can hinge on that reciprocity.

Source: Dr. Frances Edwards-Winslow, Director of Emergency Preparedness, City of San Jose, CA

8.4 Press releases

The purpose of a press release is to:

◆ Confirm the initial facts of the situation (include if video and/or audio of the event are available)
◆ Establish the organization as the authoritative source of accurate information
◆ Demonstrate actions taken to resolve the crisis
◆ Convey initial key messages

If the crisis is acute and the story is still breaking, the media will report the information from the press release immediately. If the incident is less acute, but significant, the press release will most likely generate a barrage of media inquiries and interview requests.

Press releases should have the following characteristics:

◆ **Quickly sent:** have a quick process to release the document. See section *3.4.1 Approval process to release information* and section *10.1.4 Information release clearance and parameters* for a checklist.
◆ **Complete:** release all key and relevant facts, including who, what, where, when and, if possible, why. The media will report a story with or without an organization's input.
◆ **Accurate:** include only verified information. Mistakes are nearly impossible to 'erase' completely and have a tendency to reappear at

inopportune moments. Therefore, **confirm information two and three times,** especially names and statistics.

◆ **Clear:** avoid technical jargon; if this is necessary, definitions should be included. Use declarative sentences as much as possible, such as 'The Company is operating on its regular schedule.'

◆ **Brief:** keep release length preferably one page, maximum two. Reporters do not have time to wade through reams of material. Give the media and the public information and background in the context necessary to understand the nature of the situation.

◆ **Quotes:** include statements from officials on the scene or communications staff. In the early stages of a crisis, reporters will use the quotes provided in the press release. Later, quotes from news conferences and interviews will replace the initial statements as developments occur and/or the organization releases additional information.

◆ **Contact information:** include CCT Leader office telephone, fax, e-mail, website and mailing address. Releasing home or cell phone numbers is up to the discretion of each CCT Leader.

◆ **Website:** in addition to e-mailing and/or faxing the press release, post the document on the website section dedicated to the incident

Weather forecasting

At the Miami, Florida office of the National Hurricane Center, Director Max Mayfield frequently reminds his forecasters to avoid technical terms – or at least define them – when dealing with the media and the public. "There is no reason for us to say 'convection' when we really mean thunderstorms," he says. "We're here to help people, not confuse them."

As crises frequently involve journalists who are generalists, their job requires them to learn and report the basics quickly and accurately. Therefore, the press release and all of the organization's public communications must incorporate those attributes of quick assimilation and turnaround. **If an organization makes it easy for a journalist to cover an incident, that journalist is more likely to use information directly from the organization.**

Press release template

Organization LOGO
PRESS RELEASE
[center, **BOLD**, large font]

Date:
Name: (main point of contact)
Title:
Tel:
Fax:
E-mail:
Website:

TITLE
[CENTER, BOLD, CAPS]

Paragraph 1: Who, what, where, when, why and response, whether video/audio interviews are available

Paragraph 2: Relevant background information and overall organization mission/duties

Paragraph 3: Indicate time, location of press conference or that additional information is forthcoming

End with: ### or –30–
Indicate second page: 'more'
[center]

Footer: tel, fax, e-mail, address and website

Also see section *10.2 Templates.*

8.5 Press conferences

Consider holding a press conference if there is new and significant information the organization wants to disseminate as quickly as possible. A press conference allows the spokesperson to brief all members of the media at the same time and set a timetable for the next update, both of which can help minimize the flow of press calls.

As a general rule, reserve press conferences for important announcements. The organization's most senior official should serve as the main spokesperson with relevant authorities and/or experts available to answer specific questions. The CCT Leader should manage the event but it is the senior officials from whom the media want to hear.

8.5.1 Preparation

The CCT Leader should carefully **prepare speakers, materials and media procedures** for a press conference. Even major organizations have neglected these needs. John Curran, Home Assignment Editor in the Newsgathering Department of the BBC recounts an awkward press conference experience at an airport in Glasgow, Scotland:

"Sometimes the big guys can get it so wrong when a few basic things can make it much more polished. We've nicknamed a major brand name company's announcement of a huge sports sponsorship deal 'the news conference from hell.' They failed to turn off the public address system in the room and warn us that they would be speaking only in German. They did drag a German-speaking shop assistant out of the duty-free store to interpret but failed to give him a microphone. As the main player got up to leave, the network broadcasters by agreement jumped and door-stepped him and forced him to utter a few words in English. Based on that single sound bite, we constructed a package using graphics and library film for the flagship evening news show. It was hard work to make them look at least competent, and it shouldn't have been."

◆ **Spokespeople:** a senior executive/official should serve as the spokesperson, although he/she may refer questions to other experts also present
  - Adhere to the previously approved statements and/or answers
  - Do not answer questions regarding other organizations' operations
  - If questions will be taken, prepare for possible questions, especially on **intermediate and longer-term impact of event**
  - If required, translations of official statements should immediately follow the English statement. The individual providing the translation should also be able to receive questions in that language.

- Establish how often press conferences should be held. In most cases twice a day is satisfactory. The CCT Leader or other members can provide 'routine' scheduling information as needed.

◆ **Media advisory:** issue an advisory to all media outlets by **fax, e-mail and website** to announce the event including:
  - Reason for press conference
  - Organization name and background
  - Likely speakers
  - Video or audio tape available
  - Instructions and set-up requirements for the media
  - Time and overall briefing schedule if possible or necessary
  - Location

Media advisory template

Organization LOGO
MEDIA ADVISORY
[center, **BOLD**, large font]

Date:
Name: (main point of contact)
Title:
Tel:
Fax:
E-mail:
Website:

TITLE
[CENTER, BOLD, CAPS]

Paragraph 1: Reason for press conference, speakers

Paragraph 2: Instructions for media

Paragraph 3: Indicate time, location of press conference and/or overall briefing schedule

End with: ### or –30–
Indicate second page: 'more'
[center]

Footer: tel, fax, e-mail, address and website

Also see media advisory template in section *10.2 Templates*.

◆ **Materials:** distribute written information to ensure the confirmation of as much information as possible, including:
  • Spokesperson-prepared statements issued at the beginning, especially if the spokespeople will not be taking questions
  • Media kits containing the most current statement/release, organization and incident backgrounders and other relevant materials
◆ **Visuals:** display graphs and maps on easels as appropriate
◆ **Website:** after the press conference, post above items on the section of website devoted to the incident

8.5.2 Media access
Be prepared to explain the ground rules to members of the media immediately because they may arrive on site soon after the incident occurs and before the **press conference area** and CCT **Crisis Center** are ready. John Curran, Home Assignment Editor in the Newsgathering Department of the BBC explains how the media moves quickly to obtain site access:

"On a major breaker in Britain our standard 'send', or the first wave, is three live television trucks, two radio cars, six crews, six correspondents, six producers and every dispatch rider in the building all carrying digital video cameras. Then we draw breath and say, 'What sort of breaker is this? Do we need a cherry picker, a helicopter, a Winnebago [and/or] some kind of maritime capability?' We have to move swiftly because police put so much effort into cordons that if you don't get your assets deployed and in there quick it can seriously hamper coverage."

Only allow media members with press badges to enter the media staging area. Establishing a perimeter and ground rules will:

◆ Maintain the integrity of the site for the responders to conduct their operation
◆ Ensure privacy of those affected
◆ Ensure the safety of reporters and crew

These rules may include:

◆ **Setting certain areas off-limits** because of continuing rescue efforts, investigative efforts or other security matters
◆ Informing the media of the **precise location** of all future **briefings**
◆ If possible, **establishing a regular schedule** for updates – for example, every two, four or six hours depending on the event
◆ Making it clear that any **major new developments will be shared immediately,** regardless of the schedule. This should allow the media to

US Federal Emergency Management Agency (FEMA) representative speaks to media behind perimeter during Miami-Dade (FLTF-1) Task Force search and rescue operations of a gas mainline explosion inside Humberto Vidal Building in San Juan, Puerto Rico. Source: photo by Delyris Aquino, FEMA, November 22, 1996 ***2002****/0535633*

    understand that by leaving an incident scene they may not hear the most up-to-date information.

◆ Respond to **requests for tours** of the incident site, particularly if it is a disaster site. In some cases, small groups of journalists might be allowed to make escorted visits.

◆ Consider **creating a media pool** depending on the situation. If the space limits numbers of media participants, **let the media decide which members join the pool.** (For more information see section *2.7 Creating media pool procedures.*)

◆ If the event is in **an especially unsafe area, use one of the responders trained in videography** to film footage for distribution to the media through the pool.

◆ Keep in mind special considerations, such as natural disasters, human-caused hazards or mechanical/technological malfunctions (see section *6.5 Incident-based situation assessment and considerations*)

Responding to breaking events

If events are breaking and not all the equipment is ready, only positioning the spokesperson at the press conference area site will suffice. The media will provide the necessary equipment. Be prepared to confirm the basics of the incident and the briefing schedule, if known.

Information about an incident and continuing response and recovery operations may not be available and/or confirmed. In these situations **it is acceptable and advisable to answer with what is known at that time and to explain that events are changing rapidly.** Subsequently, explain that more information will follow and announce when and where the next briefing will occur. The media understand that some time is required to assemble a complete picture. They also understand that some information will change – for instance, the number of victims, their condition or a final timeline of the event.

8.5.3 Indoor press conference area and Crisis Center

When press conferences are held indoors, put the press conference area and the Crisis Center in different rooms or on different floors. (See section *3.6.1 Crisis Center* on equipping a CCT meeting area.) If the Crisis Center is near the press conference area, consider installing entrance access codes to the Crisis Center so that media personnel passing by do not intentionally or inadvertently eavesdrop. If this is a joint operation involving public and private organizations, **private organizations may need to set up a Crisis Center in a nearby hotel or other available facility.**

Always try to **keep at least one member of the CCT in the press conference area with the media.** He or she can provide information and act as a conduit to the crisis response team for any inquiries.

Indoor press conference area equipment

Most organizations will not have a fully equipped, state-of-the-art press conference area for use in a crisis. However, the following equipment, resources and procedures should be readily available to most organizations in order to assist the media and present the organization in a positive light.

◆ Use a well-lit, cool, quiet room (be careful of acoustic problems in large gymnasium-like rooms)

◆ Ensure ready access to the outside, for stringing of media cables to satellite and live-broadcast trucks

◆ Provide a podium or microphone stand for the speakers

◆ Do not elevate the speaker; try to have the media and the podium at the same height. However, know the height of the speakers and provide a riser for short spokespeople.

◆ Use a solid backdrop color behind the speaking podium (blue is the best color for cameras)

◆ Place the organization's logo/name/seal directly behind the podium

◆ If possible, provide a series of phone lines in the back room away from the press conference area

◆ Be prepared to provide phone lines for media-only use only to avoid phone and internet disruptions. The media should maintain and pay for separate analog telephone lines, if the situation requires.

◆ On the wall, post ground rules for the media specific to the organization's technological set up and facility access

Audience-level podium with a marquee on the front and behind on a blue background. Source: Miami-Dade Fire Rescue.   ***2002***/0535635

8.5.4 Outdoors press conference area

Ideally, the Crisis Center and the press conference area should both be located on-site to ensure close proximity to the situation and to facilitate the immediate dissemination of breaking news. The Crisis Center should be isolated from the press by physical barriers and/or some distance, allowing for privacy.

If the press conference area is in the field or the incident is outdoors, consider the following:

◆   Establish a perimeter and require the press to show their credentials at the post entrance

Miami-Dade Fire Rescue (MDFR) PIOs Rhonda Barnett and Louie Fernandez convene a press conference after the 1996 ValuJet crash. Source: Miami-Dade Fire Rescue **2002**/0535634

◆ Provide a media staging area using the same type of equipment as for an indoor event: podium, backdrop, microphones and so on

◆ Situate the staging area close enough to allow members of the media to record visuals of the incident scene (unless this would put the media in danger or compromise response efforts)

◆ Inform the media and incident managers/ commanders of the location as soon as it is established

◆ Situate the Crisis Center as appropriately as possible, ideally mid-way between the incident and the press

◆ If possible, use natural barriers (roadways, canals and so on) as buffer zones between the media, the Crisis Center and the Incident Command Post

◆ Work with the producers to ensure that the site will work with media outlets intending to go live. Satellite uplink/downlink trucks must be close by to broadcast the event live.

If this is a joint operation involving public and private organizations, private organizations may need to set up a Crisis Center in a nearby hotel or other available facility. **After the initial emergency phase subsides, the Crisis Center may be moved to a nearby facility.** Throughout, it is the media's responsibility to be self-sufficient in finding their own provisions, such as food, beverages and hotels.

8.5.5 Crisis Communications Team vehicle

If an incident takes place away from an organization's base, for example at a company warehouse or in a rural area of a jurisdiction, the CCT vehicle can serve as a portable office and audio support unit.

The outdoor press conference area is intended for briefings, but the CCT Leader needs to be near the media and able to travel. Equip the designated CCT vehicle with the following:

◆ **Audio equipment:** speakers, microphones, microphone stand

◆ **Portable backdrop** and podium

◆ **Lighting equipment**
◆ **Cellular phone** with car adaptor or battery charger
◆ **Writing equipment:** paper, pens, hand-held dry erase boards
◆ **Laptop computer** with car charger, ideally with a wireless communications device to send e-mails and monitor Internet coverage
◆ **Two-way radios** to communicate with the rest of the organization. Be careful about information security when using wireless communications because the media satellite uplink/downlink trucks can often intercept radio and cell-phone exchanges.
◆ **Identifying attire:** spokesperson vest or jacket
◆ **Appropriate clothing/equipment including:**
  • Protection against the weather: sun block, insect repellent, rain gear, boots, snow suits and so on
  • Breath mints or gum
  • Mirror

8.5.6 Procedures during a press conference

The CCT Leader will manage the press conference by:

◆ Explaining the schedule, time frame for statements, question-and-answer period and/or future briefing times while standing beside the podium. **Do not step up to the microphone unless ready to go 'live' with the actual press conference.** The media is there to broadcast the principal speaker's statement, not the procedural details.

- ◆ Listing ground rules such as whether or not questions will be taken
- ◆ Introducing the speakers
- ◆ Managing the question-and-answer period if the main spokesperson does not want to select the questioners
- ◆ If there is a regular briefing schedule but a statement is not available, announce this immediately and state when the next briefing is scheduled to occur
- ◆ If the press conference will be delayed, immediately inform the media

Matchmaking

As an event unfolds and the flow of major, hard facts about the incident begins to ebb, the media will become more interested in specific details and human-interest features. They will seek assistance from the CCT Leader or members in identifying possible stories and accessing relevant information. Watch for opportunities that will help fill this need. When possible and appropriate, attempt to bring together news sources that have a story to tell with the media that can transmit those stories. This may be derived from:

- ◆ Hearing about successes in internal briefings or reading them in daily situation reports (SITREPs)
- ◆ Speaking with on-scene managers, involved employees or other witnesses

8.6 Interview guidelines

When speaking to the press, spokespersons will not have the opportunity to 'revise' any statements. Every time someone from the involved organization speaks with a journalist, that person is essentially giving an interview. Therefore, it is in an organization's interest to inform all employees on how to interact with the media. For training information see section *3.5.1 Staff training*.

8.6.1 Types of interviews

At all media organizations, including print, radio, television, and Internet, interviews have different levels of engagement:

◆ **In depth:** a news source and a reporter meet at a prearranged time and place for a formal interview. The reporter is likely to have conducted some degree of research and to have prepared questions.

◆ **Less formal:** a reporter calls a potential source at the office or home, or happens upon him/her at a crisis scene. The reporter asks a few questions, which tend to be superficial but might also be quite substantive. Even the most casual remark is on the record and could return to haunt the source.

◆ **Very informal:** interviewee and the reporter are walking from an event scene, to the parking lot or maybe they see each other at a restaurant. No notebooks or cameras are in sight.

◆ **Taped:** for 7- to 10-second sound bites; the

reporter, editor and/or producer selects the content used

◆ **Live:** for significant and breaking news; the spokesperson can speak freely

◆ **Live to tape:** usually during a remote interview; the session is live but immediately put on tape for broadcast at a later time. Although it will air as 'live,' the interviewee has an opportunity to talk to the producers to clear up any major discrepancies.

◆ **Panel:** several interviewees, typically representing different issues or perspectives. Many times there are audience questions. Being brief and calm are vital to being understood and respected.

◆ **Press conference:** for significant announcements, the speakers can present prepared statements and visuals, conduct a question-and-answer period and distribute materials

◆ **Group interview:** similar to a press conference, but more than one spokesperson presents and answers questions. Beforehand, decide who is responsible for areas the media's questions will cover.

8.6.2 Off the record

Off the record means that a reporter agrees not to attribute a statement to the spokesperson, per his or her request, and can only use the information if a second credible source independently confirms the statement. Although spokespeople and news sources cultivate relationships with journalists to manage the release of breaking information as quickly and accurately as possible, **as a rule consider everything to be on the record.** Not-for-attribution statements may jeopardize the consistency of key messages in the event the journalist breaks that trust. **To a reporter, members of an involved organization are always a news source and everything they say or do is for fair use.**

This is not to suggest avoiding all informal contacts with reporters or never speaking off the record. This would damage relationships with the media and undermine personal and organizational credibility. Speaking off the record to provide background information on an issue or incident is useful to educate the media, especially if the source is from a private organization. When events are changing quickly during emergencies, officially, however, it is safest to only speak on the record.

Always try to cement relationships with the media because informal contacts do help in disseminating accurate information quickly. Just be aware that all people serve as news sources to journalists.

Personal recordings
To ensure accuracy, spokespersons have the right to make their own recording of an in-depth interview. If a spokesperson is worried about the reporter's objectivity or skill, he or she may want to bring along a small cassette recorder and ask to be allowed to operate it him or herself. News sources do not usually do this and most reporters do not embrace the concept.

8.6.3 Interview guidelines: do's and do not's

Before agreeing to conduct an interview, review the interview details from the media log and checklist of releasable information. Some general guidelines to communicate effectively and to protect an organization's reputation during an interview include:

Interview do's

◆ Explain the scope of your comments **before the interview** and also what is interesting about the situation at hand
◆ Speak name and title; spell last name
◆ Advise the reporter of individual's role in the crisis
◆ Remember that **the public is the real audience,** not the interviewer. The spokesperson is to educate or inform the public. The interviewer is merely a conduit.

Messages

◆ **Be honest, share confirmed information.** Say, "This is what we know presently."
◆ Reinforce what the reporter should know. **Repeat key messages** to make sure they are recorded in the reporter's notes and increase the likelihood of appearing in the report.
◆ Relate key messages to the **recovery objective**
◆ **Be clear about what is not confirmed.** Say, "We have no confirmed information about that at this time. We'll share any confirmed information as soon as we receive it."

◆ **Use facts and figures** to reinforce your message. Cite outside experts, industry reports and so on.
◆ Be alert for leading questions
◆ **Break down multipart questions** and address each issue in turn
◆ Offer to clarify any points ideally during, but also after the interview

Demeanor

◆ **Speak in plain language,** using short, concise sentences
◆ Be polite, not argumentative
◆ **Maintain eye contact** with the reporter
◆ Words and body language should suggest that dealing with the media is natural and right – not a hassle, inconvenience or nerve-wracking experience

Interview do not's

Message

◆ Never lie
◆ **Do not offer personal opinions**
◆ Do not speak negatively of others' personal character
◆ **Do not place blame**
◆ **Never speculate.** Distinctions tend to fade as news makes its way from the reporter to the editor and then to the public. Often, speculation is rapidly

transformed into fact by the time it reaches the public.

◆ **Avoid information overkill.** Do not let your message be lost in a flood of peripheral information.

◆ Do not simply answer 'yes' and 'no.' **Use every response as an opportunity to deliver a key message**

◆ Avoid jargon

◆ Avoid acronyms

Approach

◆ **Do not volunteer information** when the reporter pauses before asking another question. Remain quiet and wait for the reporter to ask the next question.

◆ **Do not repeat loaded or slanted words** the questioner uses. Doing so gives double exposure to the accusation, such as "I am not a crook." Make the answer re-cast the question as positive. For example, "The company has passed all accounting audits without problems each year."

◆ **Do not use 'no comment,'** because the public often interprets it as an admission of guilt. Explain, "I have nothing for you now" and why you cannot answer the question.

Although the interview may be taped, make a best effort to give statements correctly the first time.

8.6.4 Telephone interview tips

At the outset, limit the time available for a telephone interview. There is an obligation to answer important questions from the media but save time by sending materials in advance. **Be sure to confirm whether the interview is live, live to tape or taped.**

◆ Go to a quiet room to avoid distractions
◆ If the interview is for television, keep the television on mute to see what footage the station airs, as it is sometimes not screened thoroughly. If it is for radio, having the television nearby will provide any breaking news.
◆ Confirm who is on the other end of the line
◆ Ask if the interview is being recorded
◆ Keep key messages near for quick reference. Repeat them often so that reporters realize their importance.
◆ Ask when and where the information will be used
◆ Obtain the reporter's phone number to call him/her back in the event the call is interrupted or updated information is later provided
◆ Stand up to strengthen the voice and increase alertness
◆ Spell out difficult names, technical terms, phrases
◆ Ask reporters for feedback to ensure that they understand your points

8.6.5 Live radio interview tips

A live interview is very different from a taped phone

interview. **Be sure to confirm whether the interview is live, live to tape or taped.** If the interview is live, determine if there will be callers, how callers are selected and what they will be permitted to ask.

◆ Speak in normal tones
◆ Avoid filler words such as 'uh,' 'um,' and 'you know.' Take the time to form your thoughts and answer.
◆ Use notes on hand-sized note cards but do not rustle papers. Use a highlighter to emphasize key messages.
◆ **Answer questions in 10 to 12 seconds** using key messages when appropriate
◆ Do not offer lengthy technical explanations. Remember that the audience most likely has very little technical background. **Tell them what the information means to them.** Take on the audience's point of view.
◆ Know that reporters may ask the same question multiple times in an attempt to elicit a different answer or to obtain an answer to the question with fewer words
◆ Assume the microphone is always live

8.6.6 Television interview tips

Spokespersons must take the time to prepare for an appearance. With the help of the CCT Leader or members, practice answering questions, especially aggressive, rapid-fire questions. Ideas, facts and anecdotes must be part of the spokesperson's thinking so he or she can discuss them easily and naturally. Avoid memorized answers as they might sound recited plus the interviewee needs to be flexible to be most effective. **Be sure to confirm whether the interview is live, live to tape or taped.**

◆ **Answer each question in 10 to 12 seconds** using key messages when appropriate

◆ **If a question calls for a longer answer, pause every 20 seconds.** This will make it easier for the host to break in for a commercial interruption.

◆ **Practice stopping** as the interviewer directs. Hard breaks in mid-sentence at commercials look unprofessional and desperate.

◆ **Speak slowly** and deliberately; pause between sentences to appear in control. Microphones tend to make people speak too quickly.

◆ **Drive out monotone by** raising and lowering the pitch of your voice, not the volume

◆ **Do not make broad unnatural gestures** or move around in your chair. Natural, calm animation helps increase credibility.

◆ Ask for a chair that does **not swivel**

◆ **Maintain eye contact with the reporter,** unless directed otherwise

◆ **Ensure that the earphone fits securely** and know what to do if it pops out of the ear. Ask the producer or sound/camera technician for help if needed.

◆ **Sit comfortably upright.** In a confrontational interview, the **reporter might try to sit very close**

to make the subject feel uncomfortable. Do not hesitate to ask the producer to adjust the seats before taping.

◆ **In taped interviews, ask to repeat your response** if you believe the first attempt was not your best. **In live interviews, correct misstatements** as quickly as possible.

8.7 What to wear on television

Wear clothes appropriate to the situation. In a field situation, a suit may not be appropriate. Only wear a uniform if **it is for the job.**

Men

◆ Avoid patterned suits, stripes, and checks
◆ Button double-breasted suits and single-breasted suits may be unbuttoned. If possible, sit on coattails, to avoid bunching around the neck and shoulders.
◆ White shirts are considered the most conservative. Also consider wearing light blue or gray. Bottom line: in an emergency, look conservative, not stylish or flashy.
◆ Neckties should be somber. Do not 'advertise' a product or point of view on your tie.
◆ Wear knee-length socks darker than the suit
◆ Be clean-shaven
◆ Use make-up, typically available for in-studio interviews. If the make-up technician offers make-up, take it as a sign that it is needed.

◆ Bald men should keep their heads up and consider powdering the top of their heads

Women
◆ Do not wear short skirts
◆ Wear neutral colors and muted patterns. Most set backdrops are blue or purple.
◆ Wear dark shoes
◆ Avoid distracting or shiny jewelry and any accessory that jangles or needs constant adjusting
◆ Wear everyday make-up. Avoid loud fingernail color. Lipstick should be a neutral/natural shade; lip liner helps define the lips. Women who never wear make-up should consider color on the lips.

Men and women
◆ Neat, trimmed hair is best
◆ If your skin is shiny under the lights, ask for powder
◆ Take off eye glasses unless doing so causes squinting. Consider non-glare glasses if wearing them is a must. Never wear tinted lenses or sunglasses.

Source: CDC Crisis and Emergency Risk Communication, September 2002

With proper preparation, communicating to the public through the media can convey the organization's key messages with a directed focus and in minimum time.

Working with the media's time constraints and responding to their information needs best serves the crisis response efforts.

CHAPTER 9: POST-INCIDENT MANAGEMENT

CHAPTER 9: POST-INCIDENT MANAGEMENT

9.1 Last remaining updates

After the initial, continuing and diminishing stages of a crisis pass, several events can create surges of activity or interest. Some newsworthy updates to the incident include (but are not limited to):

◆ Final details and resolution of the event, people involved
◆ Additional survivors/casualties
◆ Developments in an investigation, or legal developments such as the filing of a lawsuit or criminal charges
◆ Seasonal expectations, including hurricane or brush fire season

9.2 End of the crisis

Once it is clear that the crisis has ended, follow these post-incident steps:

◆ **Declare an end to the crisis:** upon confirmation, signal an end to the crisis situation
  • Announcing a **completed search and rescue** to the families of victims is a very traumatic experience for everyone involved – including the CCT and responders. With the utmost certainty, ensure final confirmation from the response team before announcing this **first to the families** and then to the press. (See section *7.12 Understanding the psychological effects of*

> *a crisis* for guidance on forming messages with empathy and compassion.)

◆ **Follow up with stakeholders:** stay in touch with the affected groups and individuals after a crisis, especially those directly affected. Keep the media informed of any updates in the situation.

◆ **Perform an act of goodwill:** do this during or immediately after a crisis, when appropriate and possible, to display commitment beyond self-preservation within the crisis resolution process

◆ **Conduct a Post-Incident Analysis (PIA):** analyze the incident outcome and media coverage, both positive and negative. Institute a mechanism to improve planning and future response procedures.

9.3 Conduct a Post-Incident Analysis (PIA)

A PIA is an important tool in continuing training of the Crisis Communications Team (CCT). Ideally, **the PIA is an exercise for all members of the crisis response team(s) to reflect on the events** as they transpired, and to communicate ideas for policy and procedure improvement. By completing a 'cross-section' PIA that includes other departments, the organization will gain knowledge of the roles and responsibility of the CCT as a part of the crisis response team. The outcome of a PIA is for the Team Leader to manage the implementation of any changes that would improve CCT procedures.

Complete the PIA as soon as possible after the crisis, using these guidelines:

- ◆ The CCT Leader should assemble all participants from the response as soon as possible, while memories are clear
- ◆ Conduct the entire PIA in a single meeting
- ◆ Emphasize to all participants that the PIA is a fact-finding exercise to improve future planning and response procedures. It is not an occasion to argue, degrade or belittle.
- ◆ Recount incident events chronologically
- ◆ Identify responsibility for participants' actions
- ◆ Identify shortcomings
- ◆ Identify areas for improvement
- ◆ Establish timelines to implement proposed changes
- ◆ Distribute findings and recommendations to relevant department managers, supervisors and/or other partnering organizations

9.4 Healing events and anniversaries

The CCT will most likely need to coordinate events commemorating, remembering or acknowledging the past crisis. These events will most likely be public relations events for the organization and the community. It is important to remember that the organization serves a role in the community and the community will expect organization representatives to participate.

Each case will be different, but use these guidelines to organize event logistics:

- ◆ What is the ceremonial objective?

- ◆ Who will be participating?
- ◆ What will be the role of the organization?
- ◆ Who will be the lead coordinating entity?
- ◆ What resources will be allocated to the event?
- ◆ What is the timeframe: for preparation and for the event?
- ◆ What are the individual responsibilities:
  - Press
  - Liaisons
  - Logistics
  - Communications
  - Volunteer, charitable offers
  - High-level officials, celebrities
  - Participants
  - Counselors to address emotional responses, if necessary

9.4.1 Publicizing the event

Since the commemoration is related to the original event, the organization needs to continue to display its dedication to issues surrounding the past crisis.

Using the contact information archived in the media log from the original incident, invite the media and involved stakeholders of the event in a press release and on the organization's website, as soon as details are confirmed. Include the following:

- ◆ Praise the response and recovery effort
- ◆ Honor losses of the community

◆ Provide information on **trauma recovery** for victims, families, public and response workers

See section *7.12 Understanding the psychological effects of a crisis* for more information.

9.4.2 Media relations
The media will usually respond to these events. The reporters who attend, however, may not be the same people who covered the original crisis or event. The reporter may have changed jobs or the assignment editor may choose to dispatch a different reporter. Consider these proactive communications steps:

◆ Include in the press releases and other material relevant details about the original event, including human-interest anecdotes from the response effort
◆ Pre-clear media to coordinate the event smoothly, with sensitivity to the attendees and for security reasons, if necessary
◆ Consider forming a media pool if there is a high interest and/or the anniversary surrounds a sensitive event

Anniversary of 9/11 in New York
The one-year anniversary of September 11 was a worldwide event for New York City. Balancing the sensitivities of family members and world leaders, access for 300 media outlets, the constraints of the World Trade Center site and tight security presented an enormous challenge. Ten government agencies and 12

private and charitable organizations provided logistical and technical accommodations for the media. The six-month commemoration and the May 30 ceremony of the recovery end gave the organizers valuable logistical experience.

Starting in mid-July, the Mayor's Press Office led media planning with New York Police Department (NYPD) and Office of Emergency Management (OEM) press offices. They handled thousands of media requests: 40 percent television, 30 percent photo, 20 percent print and 10 percent radio. They established 17 different media pools requiring a contact from each outlet to work with the Mayor's Press Office. With cooperation from Merrill Lynch, Dow Jones and Brookfield Properties, they provided the media access to rooftops for coverage.

To ensure security, the Mayor's Press Office worked with the NYPD, OEM and the Port Authority Police Department. All media, including crew and interview guests, with valid credentials were pre-approved for access – a process requiring significant planning time. The NYPD managed scanning all bags and a 24-hour security detail.

The media coverage was incredibly successful because of inter-agency coordination and public-private partnerships.

Source: information provided by the New York Mayor's Press Office: Ed Skyler, Press Secretary; Megan Sheekey, Deputy Press Secretary and Jennifer Falk, Deputy Press Secretary

CHAPTER 10: APPENDICES

CHAPTER 10: APPENDICES

10.1 Response procedures checklists

10.1.1 Initial phase

Initial phase

☐ Team Leader notifies senior leadership

☐ Assemble Crisis Communications Team

☐ Dispatch team member(s) to site: researcher, video/photo, translator

☐ Clear initial press release

☐ Fax, e-mail press release to press on media contact list

☐ Identify initial spokespersons on team

☐ Respond to initial media inquiries by phone

☐ Assign duties to Crisis Communications Team

    ☐ Information liaisons: site, stakeholders, partners, subject matter experts (internal or external)

    ☐ Researcher

    ☐ Media queries/media log maintenance

    ☐ Media monitoring

☐ Editor/writer

☐ Website

☐ Crisis Center and press conference area

☐ Assess the gravity of the crisis, contact families/key stakeholders

☐ Arrange VIP visits (could occur during all phases)

10.1.2 Continuing phase

Continuing phase

☐ Establish Joint Information Center (JIC), if necessary

☐ Consider incident-specific responses

☐ Create key messages

☐ Announce/prepare for press conference

    ☐ Send out media advisory to press on media contact list

    ☐ Identify speakers, prepare their talking points

    ☐ Create visuals, press kits

    ☐ Identify language requirements

☐ Establish media perimeter around the site

☐ Set up press conference area

    ☐ Podium

- □ Equipment: microphones, speakers, camera, recording, lighting, phone/internet lines
- □ Organization banner/marquee
□ Conduct interviews
□ Monitor media coverage
□ Create media pool, release video/photos
□ Set up schedule for next day or for 24-hour schedule
    - □ Additional logistical support
    - □ Meetings: communications/response units
    - □ Interviews and press conferences

10.1.3 Diminishing, resolution, evaluation and recognition phases

Diminishing phase

□ Re-assemble Crisis Communications Team
    - □ Assess situation
    - □ Discuss media coverage
□ Pursue corrections, if necessary
□ Send out updated press release
□ Prepare for second press conference

- ☐ Respond to new inquiries, interview requests
- ☐ Coordinate volunteer offers

Resolution phase

- ☐ Declare end to crisis
  - ☐ Send out press release or announce press conference, if making a significant announcement
- ☐ Summarize key messages
- ☐ Follow up with key constituents

Evaluation phase

- ☐ Conduct Post-Incident Analysis with Crisis Communications Team and/or entire crisis response team

Recognition phase

- ☐ Arrange memorial events, anniversaries
- ☐ Publicize event and provide materials

10.1.4 Information release clearance and parameters

Information clearance procedures

- ☐ Verified all information
- ☐ Includes answers to outside queries

- ☐ Includes key messages
- ☐ Is 'headline' material
- ☐ Cleared by Team Leader
- ☐ Cleared by respective operations manager
-   Cleared by subject matter expert

Information protected: not for release

- ☐ Classified material
- ☐ Law enforcement evidence
- ☐ Covered by statute
- ☐ Victims, families, employees, responders' privacy
  - ☐ Name, age, marital status, contact information, residence, health history/status, deployment location (military)
- ☐ Proprietary
- ☐ Business confidential
- ☐ Internal discussion: memoranda, e-mail

10.2 Templates

10.2.1 Media log

Date:	**Time:**
Organization name:	
Type of media (circle): wire print TV radio Internet	
Reporter name:	
Producer/editor name:	
Tel:	
Fax:	
E-mail:	
Deadline:	
Interview (circle): live taped call-in on-site in-studio	
Interview times/dates:	
Inquiry details:	
Responded to call: Date:	**Time:**

10.2.2 Press release

Organization LOGO
PRESS RELEASE
[center, **BOLD**, large font]

Date:
Name: (main point of contact)
Title:
Tel:
Fax:
E-mail:
Website:

TITLE
[CENTER, BOLD, CAPS]

Paragraph 1: Who, what, where, when, why and response, whether video/audio materials are available

Paragraph 2: Relevant background information and overall organization mission/duties

Paragraph 3: Indicate time, location of press conference or that additional information is forthcoming

End with: ### or –30–
Indicate second page: 'more'
[center]

Footer: tel, fax, e-mail, address and website

10.2.3 Media advisory

Organization LOGO
MEDIA ADVISORY
[center, **BOLD**, large font]

Date:
Name: (main point of contact)
Title:
Tel:
Fax:
E-mail:
Website:

TITLE
[CENTER, BOLD, CAPS]

Paragraph 1: Reason for press conference, speakers

Paragraph 2: Instructions for media

Paragraph 3: Indicate time, location of press conference
and/or overall briefing schedule

End with: ### or –30–
Indicate second page: 'more'
[center]

Footer: tel, fax, e-mail, address and website

10.3 Safety procedures for media

Members of the media who are assigned to cover incidents involving hazardous materials may be exposed to contaminants that could cause serious injury. In addition, investigative reporting can put journalists in dangerous environments. The organization and the media should seek out and heed the advice of the community's hazardous materials team. **If available, have responders trained in videography and photography provide pool coverage of dangerous sites.** Some laws require hazardous materials response teams to be geographically available. These teams are highly trained and can provide data and life safety help for those that need it.

At any hazardous materials scene there are three standard areas in which emergency operations personnel operate:

◆ **Hot zone:** most dangerous area, reserved for fully protected emergency responders
◆ **Warm zone:** a middle point where emergency responders prepare to enter the hot zone
◆ **Cold zone:** area reserved for bystanders, the press and others

Always respect/enforce scene perimeters set up by emergency responders.

NOTES

NOTES

NOTES

NOTES

<u>NOTES</u>

NOTES

NOTES

NOTES

NOTES

NOTES

NOTES

NOTES

NOTES